COLD ★ WAR
KANSAS

COLD ★ WAR KANSAS

LANDRY BREWER

FOREWORD BY MARK PARILLO

THE
History
PRESS

Published by The History Press
Charleston, SC
www.historypress.com

First published 2020

Manufactured in the United States

ISBN 9781467146630

Library of Congress Control Number: 2020934363

For Erin, Dylan, Kelsey, MacKinley, Quinn and Spence

CONTENTS

FOREWORD

I had never set foot in Kansas—or anyplace close—until I came out to interview for a job some three decades ago. I was fortunate enough to get that job and have lived in the Sunflower State ever since, happily raising a family and getting to know my adopted home and the people who live here.

Like most Americans who have never been here, when I first arrived, my head was filled with hazy images of small-town life and sun-bleached fields stretching to the horizon, marred perhaps by the occasional twister or two. This last vestige of pastoral America, I imagined, might still be peopled with the friendly but hardworking Auntie Ems and Uncle Henrys raising their own little Dorothys in the plain but honest goodness of the heartland. I did come to find all of that in Kansas, though, in truth, Kansas and its people are more rich and complex, as well as more beautiful and authentic, than all the popular culture stereotypes.

It is this Kansas, the real-life-is-better-than-fiction version, that Professor Brewer explores in a well-researched and fluidly written volume. The book is satisfying in its coverage of the many national political and cultural events, federal government policies, and citizen programs to endure the Cold War's existential threat to American society. But its real strength is showing how all of this played out among my fellow Kansans, the three-dimensional Kansans I have come to know and appreciate over the years.

The Cold War touched Kansas in a wide variety of ways and areas of life. Some were direct and predictable, such as the enhanced roles and responsibilities of the state's major military installations: Forbes, Schilling and McConnell Air Force Bases and Forts Leavenworth and Riley. The state's geographically central location coupled with the lower population density typical of the Midwest also made Kansas a natural choice for many of the ICBM launch sites so prominent in early Cold War defense strategy. These were an economic boost to local communities but also instilled a genuine pride among Kansans in the high priority they earned on the Soviet target list. Civil defense was another facet of the Cold War that reverberated throughout the state: defense shelters, school and community evacuation and medical treatment plans, jousting among local, state, and federal governments about funding and policy.

And Kansas played a reciprocal role in shaping the Cold War. Dwight D. Eisenhower, a favorite son of the Sunflower State, served a full two terms in the White House during the Cold War's earliest stages, establishing indispensable policies, procedures and institutions that allowed the United States, and the world at large, to survive those dangerous decades. Professor Brewer also relates the remarkable story of *The Day After*, a movie made in Kansas about Kansas in a nuclear holocaust—and a movie that shook the nation's psyche and directly influenced national policy.

Yes, this is the story of the friends, colleagues, and neighbors I have come to know in what is now my home, my Kansas, and how they weathered the dangers, the opportunities and the fortunes of the Cold War. But most of all, it is a story of Americans, and one that all Americans should know.

—Mark Parillo

Mark Parillo is an author and history professor at Kansas State University in Manhattan, Kansas.

ACKNOWLEDGEMENTS

I owe a debt of gratitude to The History Press for publishing this book. Thank you for seeing the value in it.

Acquisitions editor Chad Rhoad showed great patience with my frequent questions and photographic ignorance.

Virgil Dean with the Kansas Historical Society edited and improved a portion of the manuscript.

The SWOSU administration and my colleagues there continue to be supportive in my teaching, research and writing.

Thank you to Dr. Brad Lookingbill for your encouragement and example of scholarship, professionalism and what a kid from Elk City, Oklahoma, can accomplish.

My family continues to be a source of inspiration, in spite of their weariness with my talk of missiles, fallout shelters and all things Cold War.

INTRODUCTION

The Cold War was frightening. For more than four decades, Americans feared that civilization would end amid fire and fallout if the Cold War between the United States and the Soviet Union got hot. Kansans understood the raw power of the elements, and they understood that they were in the bullseye.

After victory in World War II, the United States found itself the leader of the free world. The Soviet Union's Red Army had marched into eastern Europe en route to Berlin to force a Nazi surrender. Where the Red Army went, Communism followed. Millions of Poles, Germans, Czechs and others found themselves enslaved under Communist rule, puppet states controlled by Moscow.

To Americans, Joseph Stalin had replaced Adolf Hitler as the dictator trying to conquer Europe and the world. Because no other nation in the world had the ability to intervene and stop Soviet expansion, American foreign policy in the late 1940s changed with the intent of stopping Communism's march.

In 1947, President Truman announced that the United States would stop Communism's attempt to undermine and control free people with economic, political and, if necessary, military assistance. The latter included the atomic bomb.

The nation—including Kansas—readied itself for what President Kennedy called a "long twilight struggle."

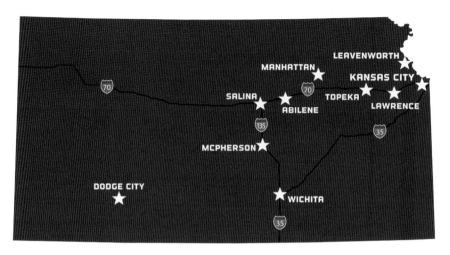

Kansas map locating ten of the cities featured prominently in state Cold War activities. *Courtesy of Southwestern Oklahoma State University graphics designer Kyle Wright.*

From the four corners of the state, Kansans joined national efforts to bolster national security and stop Communism as the Soviet Union appeared intent on conquering our European allies and further spreading its influence. With its acquiring thermonuclear weapons and the ability to deliver them, that nation also appeared intent on attacking the United States and inflicting possibly civilization-ending destruction.

Kansans from all walks of life sprang into action. Some military bases in the state were opened, and others were expanded. Long-range missile sites were built and operated. Civilians prepared to survive the effects of a nuclear attack. State and national politicians from Kansas readied their governments to protect their constituents and preserve the nation's way of life in the face of grave—and at times imminent—danger.

The Cold War was dangerous. For the world. For the nation. For Kansas.

This book tells an important story. It reminds us that the world became extremely dangerous and remained so for more than four decades, when nations with nuclear weapons at their disposal came close to using them against each other.

And it reminds us of Kansas's important role then.

In a 1961 speech to the United Nations, as the Cold War was in its most dangerous era, President Kennedy said, "Every man, woman and child lives under a nuclear sword of Damocles, hanging by the slenderest of threads, capable of being cut at any moment by accident or miscalculation or by madness."[1]

Kansans did what they could to keep family members, friends, neighbors and constituents safe. They built missile sites and lived with nuclear-armed missiles. They taught citizens how to install fallout shelters. They served in the military. They served in the government. They even acted in an influential made-for-TV movie. For forty-five years, Kansans fought the long twilight struggle hoping the sword of Damocles would never fall.

The four-plus decades of danger were, perhaps, more tangible for Kansas than they were for the rest of the nation. This book explains why. This book tells Kansas's Cold War story.

1

COLD WAR ORIGINS

Though the United States and the Soviet Union were allies during World War II, the two nations became adversaries when the war ended in 1945.[2] The Nazi military had taken control of Eastern Europe by the end of 1941. When the war ended four years later, the Red Army, having defeated the German army on its march to Berlin, controlled that territory for the Soviet Union. "The Soviet Union occupied East Europe. This crucial result of World War II destroyed the Grand Alliance and gave birth to the Cold War," according to historians Stephen Ambrose and Douglas Brinkley.[3]

At the February 1945 Yalta Conference, three months before World War II ended in Europe with Germany's surrender, leaders of the United States, Great Britain and the Soviet Union—Franklin Roosevelt, Winston Churchill and Joseph Stalin, respectively—agreed to postwar arrangements in Europe. In return for the Soviet Union joining the war against Japan within three months of Germany's surrender, Roosevelt and Churchill consented to allow the Soviet Union to exert control over Eastern Europe—but only if Stalin promised to allow free elections there. Stalin agreed. However, Stalin "never accepted the Western interpretation of the Yalta agreements."[4] The Soviet Union controlled Eastern Europe and did not intend to relinquish that control.

The United States dropped two atomic bombs on the Japanese cities Hiroshima and Nagasaki in August 1945. Shortly thereafter, the Japanese government surrendered, and World War II ended. As conditions between the former war allies worsened and the Soviet Union consolidated control over much of Europe, former British prime minister Winston Churchill played the role of prophet when he delivered a March 5, 1946 speech in President Truman's home state at Westminster College in Fulton, Missouri, with the president seated nearby. In what is now known as the "Iron Curtain" speech, Churchill said this about Soviet control of the eastern portion of a divided Europe:

> *From Stettin in the Baltic to Trieste in the Adriatic an iron curtain has descended across the continent. Behind that line lie all the capitals of the ancient states of Central and Eastern Europe. Warsaw, Berlin, Prague, Vienna, Budapest, Belgrade, Bucharest and Sofia; all these famous cities and the populations around them lie in what I must call the Soviet sphere, and all are subject, in one form or another, not only to Soviet influence but to a very high and in some cases increasing measure of control from Moscow.*[5]

By 1947, President Truman's foreign policy toward the Soviet Union and Communism had intensified. State Department official William C. Bullitt gave a mid-1947 speech at the National War College in which he likened Stalin to Hitler and said that the Soviet Union wanted to conquer the world. Communists threatened to replace the British-supported Greek government, though British aid and forty thousand British troops in Greece were preventing that from happening. When the British government informed the Americans in February 1947 that no further aid would be forthcoming and British troops would soon return home, President Truman decided that the United States must intervene. He believed that if Greece fell to Communism, its neighbor Turkey, which had been pressured by the Soviet Union to allow it a military presence there, would be next to fall. On March 12, 1947, President Truman addressed a joint session of Congress, appealing for American aid for both countries, announcing the Truman Doctrine: "I believe that it must be the policy of the United States to support free peoples who are resisting attempted subjugation by armed minorities or by outside pressures."[6]

Congress granted Truman's request with $400 million in aid for Greece and Turkey, and the United States began a new era. "For the first time in its history, the United States had chosen to intervene during a period of general peace in the affairs of peoples outside North and South America."[7] President Truman articulated the American government's new policy of containment, through which the nation sought to stop the spread of Soviet Communism.

According to Truman biographer David McCullough, American policy toward the Soviet Union changed markedly after Secretary of State George Marshall returned from a 1947 meeting with his European counterparts. Marshall told Truman that the United States could not deal with the Soviets and diplomacy was destined to fail. By late 1947, the conflict between the United States and the Soviet Union was being called the "Cold War" by columnist Walter Lippmann. Though the expression had been used earlier, Lippmann was the first to attach it to the increasingly hostile East-West divide.[8]

Secretary Marshall returned on Saturday, April 26, 1947, shocked by what he had seen in Berlin and Western Europe during his trip, which included a visit to Moscow for talks with the Soviet government. Slow to recover economically from the ravages of World War II, Western Europe was teetering on the brink of economic collapse and needed to be rescued. Marshall instructed his State Department to formulate a plan to give economic aid that would help revive Europe's economy. "Millions of people were slowly starving. A collapse in Europe would mean revolution and a tailspin for the American economy."[9] Marshall announced the European Recovery Program—its goal to help prevent economic collapse and starvation, ensure that the United States had economically viable trading partners in Europe and stave off a Communist takeover of Western Europe—during a June 5 speech at Harvard in which he announced the plan's intent:

> *Our policy is directed not against any country or doctrine, but against hunger, poverty, desperation and chaos. Its purpose should be the revival of a working economy in the world so as to permit the emergence of political and social conditions in which free institutions can exist.*[10]

The amount requested for what came to be called the Marshall Plan was $17 billion. Fearing Congress would refuse to appropriate the money, President Truman met with Speaker of the House Sam Rayburn to sell the idea. "Truman said there was no way of telling how many hundreds of thousands of people would starve to death in Europe and that this must not happen, not if it could be prevented." The president "was also sure… that if Europe went 'down the drain' in a depression, the United States would follow." He said to the speaker that they had "'both lived through one depression, and we don't want to have to live through another one, do we, Sam?'" The Marshall Plan was passed by the Congress almost one year after Marshall's Harvard speech, in April 1948.[11]

The National Security Act of 1947 was also important for American Cold War military operations and foreign policy. President Truman sent the bill to Congress for its consideration in February to reorganize the nation's military so that its several branches were all brought under the oversight "of a single Department of Defense and a single Secretary of Defense." In addition to creating the DOD, the legislation also created a separate air force, removing it from the army. The act also created the National Security Council and the Central Intelligence Agency.[12]

The eastern portion of Berlin had been occupied by the Soviets, with the Americans, British and French in the western portion of the city since World War II ended, each country within its own sector. In the summer of 1948, Joseph Stalin ordered a blockade of Berlin to prevent the Western powers from gaining access to the city by ground or water transport in an attempt to starve the democracies into submission and force them out of the city. Opinions within the American government differed as to what the country's response should be, though President Truman was adamant that the United States stand its ground. Army Chief of Staff Omar Bradley recommended to President Truman that access to West Berlin could be gained by air. Soon, "air transport… flying round-the-clock missions into Berlin, supplying up to 13,000 tons of goods per day" commenced, and "the Berlin airlift caught the imagination of the world."[13] With the airlift lasting just under one year before Stalin finally called it off in 1949,

> *official U.S. Air Force numbers include*[d]*: total cargo delivered to Berlin—2,325,809 tons, 1,783,573 of those by the Air Force and 542,236 tons by the Royal Air Forces of Britain, Australia and New Zealand, along with private aircraft chartered by the British government. The total number of flights into Berlin was recorded as 277,569—189,963 by the Americans, and 87,606 by the British and their Commonwealth partners.*[14]

The triumph of the Berlin airlift overlapped with another diplomatic triumph: the North Atlantic Treaty Organization (NATO). Delivering his inaugural address after winning the 1948 presidential election, Truman "pledged…to aid those European nations willing to defend themselves." Carrying out the president's wishes, Secretary of State Dean Acheson brokered the North Atlantic Treaty, which was signed on April 4, 1949, in Washington, D.C. "Britain, France, Belgium, the Netherlands, Italy,

Portugal, Denmark, Iceland, Norway, Canada, and the United States pledged themselves to mutual assistance in case of aggression against any of the signatories."[15] NATO was born, furthering the cause of containment in Europe.

Any feelings of triumph were overwhelmed by concern as summer became fall in 1949. In early September, a U.S. Air Force plane discovered radioactivity over the northern Pacific Ocean. On Monday, September 19, the scientists who reviewed the radioactive samples that had been gathered concluded that the Soviet Union had, for the first time, detonated an atomic bomb. The American atomic monopoly had ended. President Truman was informed the next day. He released a statement to the press Friday, September 23, informing the American public, and though there was no panic in the country, the fears and tensions of the Cold War were greatly amplified. It was a different world now."[16]

Early the next month, the years-long Chinese civil war fought between Communists led by Mao Tse-tu-ng and Nationalists led by American ally Chiang Kai-shek came to an end. Although the United States had spent billions of dollars supporting Chiang in hopes of staving off Communism's advances in China since World War II ended, it was not enough. Just one week after President Truman informed the American people that the Soviet Union had acquired its own atomic bomb, "the People's Republic of China, the most numerous Communist nation in the world, with more than 500 million people, one fifth of humanity, was officially inaugurated."[17]

That same month, October 1949, the Cold War intensified yet again. Soon after President Truman informed the nation that the Soviets had the atomic bomb, American officials began to discuss pursuing "a thermonuclear or hydrogen weapon—a superbomb, or 'Super'—which would have more than ten times the destructive power of the bombs dropped on Hiroshima and Nagasaki."[18] The belief was that if the Soviets had the capacity to build an atomic bomb, they would likely have the means and desire to create their own thermonuclear bomb, which meant that the United States must also have this weapon. President Truman agreed with his advisors who followed this logic, and on January 31, 1950, he officially signed off on developing the hydrogen—or thermonuclear—bomb.

Because of Communist ascendancy in China, the Soviet acquisition of the atomic bomb and the specter of a Soviet thermonuclear bomb—and the domestic political pressure that these events created—on January 30, 1950, President Truman tasked the Department of State and the Department of Defense with reviewing the nation's defense and foreign policy. A report was prepared, forwarded to the National Security Council and then delivered to the president as National Security Council Paper No. 68, or simply NSC 68. The report advocated a massive military buildup in an effort to offset Communist gains and discourage further Soviet expansion. It predicted that "the Soviets would probably achieve nuclear equality by 1954," and although "no cost estimates were included, the figures discussed with Truman ranged from $40 to $50 billion a year, at least three times the current military budget." The report ended ominously: "'The whole success hangs ultimately on recognition by this government, the American people and all the peoples that the Cold War is in fact a real war in which the survival of the world is at stake."[19]

That summer, Communist North Korean troops invaded South Korea. The United States would fight a three-year war trying to restore the status quo ante bellum and prevent a Communist takeover of the southern half of the Korean Peninsula. Then, in the 1960s, Americans began fighting another war, a decade-long conflict in Southeast Asia, to prevent a Communist takeover in South Vietnam. Between the two Cold War–inspired hot conflicts, the United States and the Soviet Union would reach the brink of nuclear war, each with long-range bombers and ballistic missiles that could fly thousands of miles with nuclear bombs capable of inflicting civilization-ending destruction. Then, as the 1970s became the 1980s, the nuclear arms race between the United States and the Soviet Union resumed, and new fears of nuclear war emerged. Throughout these decades, Americans—including Kansans—hoped for the best but prepared for the worst. The Cold War ushered in a different world, indeed.

2

KANSAS MISSILES

As the Soviet Union appeared to surpass American nuclear capability in the late 1950s, the United States government moved quickly to reassert its nuclear dominance.[20] That nuclear dominance was on display in the early 1960s in Kansas as several locations near Forbes Air Force Base, Schilling Air Force Base and McConnell Air Force Base operated intercontinental ballistic missiles (ICBMs) as part of the nation's offensive nuclear arsenal. Additionally, the state operated defensive antiaircraft missile sites to protect one of the state's most important cities against possible attack. Housing those missiles required massive construction projects that provided thousands of individuals with jobs and infused the state with large sums of money, which was welcomed by many Kansans, who learned to live with nuclear weapons in their midst. Most importantly, those ICBMs fortified the nation's nuclear deterrent, and antiaircraft missiles defended Americans during the Cold War's most dangerous years.

ATLAS

During Dwight Eisenhower's presidency (1953–61), American defense policy relied heavily on the nation's nuclear arsenal deterring Soviet aggression against the United States or its allies. President Eisenhower assumed office wanting to spend less money than his predecessor on national defense by reducing conventional forces and their costs. Instead, Eisenhower believed that the nation could get more for its money while maintaining its security by responding to Soviet threats against the United States and its allies with threats of nuclear retaliation. Called the "New Look" by the administration and "Massive Retaliation" by the media, Eisenhower's policy of nuclear deterrence relied on American nuclear superiority.[21]

Central to this deterrence was development of ICBMs. The nation's first ICBM was the Atlas. Development of the Atlas missile had begun by the early mid-1950s, but things changed dramatically when the Soviet Union announced that it had successfully launched the world's first ICBM in August 1957 and launched the Sputnik satellite just two months later. Pressure quickly mounted on the American government to complete the Atlas project. The Cold War power balance had shifted dramatically in 1949 when the Soviet Union acquired an atomic bomb, and the power balance appeared to radically shift again eight years later. The United States scrambled to right the perceived imbalance.[22]

Convair Astronautics, later made a division of General Dynamics, began work on the Atlas in the early 1950s. Though only ten employees were assigned to the ballistic missile project in 1953, 12,000 employees worked on the Atlas program in the company's San Diego facility in 1960. "Reflecting the truly national scope of the Atlas program," wrote John C. Lonnquest and David F. Winkler in the Department of Defense document *To Defend and Deter: The Legacy of the United States Cold War Missile Program*, "Convair employed 30 major subcontractors, 500 lesser contractors, and 5,000 suppliers scattered across 32 states."[23]

Six versions of the Atlas missile were produced: the A, B, and C were test models, and the D, E and F were deployed and operational. The Atlas missile was 82.5 feet long and 10.0 feet wide and weighed 18,104 pounds empty and 267,136 pounds when filled with liquid fuel. In flight, the missile reached speeds of 16,000 miles per hour, allowing it to travel nearly 7,000 miles in just 43 minutes, landing within 2 nautical miles of its target. Upon arrival, the Atlas's warhead would deliver a 4-megaton yield. To put this into perspective, each Atlas missile in Kansas would have delivered a nuclear bomb more than 200 times more powerful than the atomic bombs dropped by the United States on the Japanese cities Hiroshima and Nagasaki at the end of World War II.[24]

The air force used several criteria to determine the locations of ICBM launch sites. Each location had to be within the continental United States, close enough for the missile to reach its intended target, but also outside the range of Soviet missiles launched from submarines. Finally, the air force secretary ordered that, if possible, launch sites be on government property, ideally in an area with a population of at least fifty thousand. Believing that the launch sites would be targeted by the Soviet Union in the event of war, they were placed with sufficient distance between each to prevent multiple installations from being disrupted by a single Soviet bomb.[25]

The air force used the U.S. Army Corps of Engineers to build the launch complexes. The corps tasked nearby engineer districts with construction. The job proved difficult because of the immediate and intense nature of the program, especially after fall 1957, when the ICBM program was accelerated. The air force increased the number of Atlas squadrons that it would deploy. Even though the launch sites became more complex, making them increasingly difficult and costly to build, they were, however, to be built as quickly as possible. Adding to these difficulties was the method used by the air force known as the "concept of concurrency"—ICBMs were being developed and tested, while the corps simultaneously built the missile launch complexes. An air force missile design change could require the Army Corps of Engineers to change the missile sites it was building, including destroying and removing what had just been built, and starting anew. By April 1962, the Army Corps of Engineers had approved more than 2,600 Atlas launch-site modifications during construction. These modifications cost an additional $96 million, which was 40 percent more than the initial contract amount. Because of the perceived need to deploy ICBMs as quickly as possible, deployment speed trumped cost, and the concurrency method was used.[26]

Three air force bases operated nine Atlas E sites each near Fairchild Air Force Base in Washington, F.E. Warren Air Force Base in Wyoming and Forbes Air Force Base near Topeka. Topeka learned in October 1958 that Forbes AFB would operate the Atlas E missile and that nine launch sites would be built in nearby locations. The Corps of Engineers Kansas City District oversaw construction of the nine horizontal sites, dubbed "coffins," that housed nine Atlas E missiles. Originally, Forbes was scheduled to operate only three sites with three missiles located at each site, but the air force decided to diffuse the missiles at nine separate launch sites. These launch sites were located in the vicinity of Bushong, Delia, Dover, Holton, Osage City, Overbrook, Valley Falls, Waverly and Wamego. Site construction began on June 9, 1959, with a formal ceremony that included Kansas governor George Docking. The horizontal, semi-hard coffin complexes made of reinforced concrete that housed the Atlas E missiles were buried underground with aboveground retractable roofs that would expose the missile during a launch and provided blast protection for the missile up to overpressure of twenty-five pounds per square inch (psi). Each missile, the necessary support equipment and facilities were located beneath the ground in the missile launch and service building, a structure 105 feet by 100 feet. The launch sequence meant that the roof would be retracted and the missile raised to the upright position, after which it would be fueled prior to firing. The large launch operations building housed the launch control center, where an air force crew lived, and a power plant. Atlas E launch sites were separated from each other by about twenty miles.[27]

Two separate firms constructed the Atlas E sites. The difficulties that crews faced included 519 site modifications required under the concurrency construction program. Additionally, 22 work stoppages slowed site construction, though most delayed work only briefly. Though 25 on-site work accidents occurred, the most serious of these resulted in only two fatalities, both due to electrocution. The 548th Strategic Missile Squadron at Forbes AFB stood up on July 1, 1960, and the first Atlas E missile was brought to the base on January 24, 1961. All nine Atlas E missiles had arrived by the following October, and work was completed at all Forbes sites three weeks before deadline. Major General Gerrity, air force ballistic missile activation chief, transferred control of all the Forbes-area sites to Lieutenant General John D. Ryan, second air force commander, on October 16, 1961.[28]

The most sophisticated among the Atlas missiles, the Atlas F was created to be housed in deep, hardened underground silos to protect them against possible Soviet nuclear attack. Constructed of the strongest concrete possible, each silo was 174 feet deep with a diameter of 52 feet and entirely below ground. Each silo housed a missile along with an extensive steel structure, the crib—which was attached to the silo walls by four extremely large springs—that allowed for routine missile maintenance. Connected to the silo by a 50-foot-long, 8-foot-wide tunnel was the launch control center. Also built of reinforced concrete, the underground structure housed the equipment to fire the missile. To do so, the missile would be raised with an elevator through the silo top and then launched. Of all of the Atlas missile sites, the F series were the most difficult and expensive to build.[29]

To oversee the mammoth task of building several ICBM sites around the nation, the army created the Corps of Engineers Ballistic Missile Construction Office, or CEBMCO, in August 1960. One of CEBMCO's goals was to provide continuity and consistency through centralized control in building missile sites. According to Lonnquest and Winkler, "To do that, CEBMCO's commanding officer appointed weapon system directors for

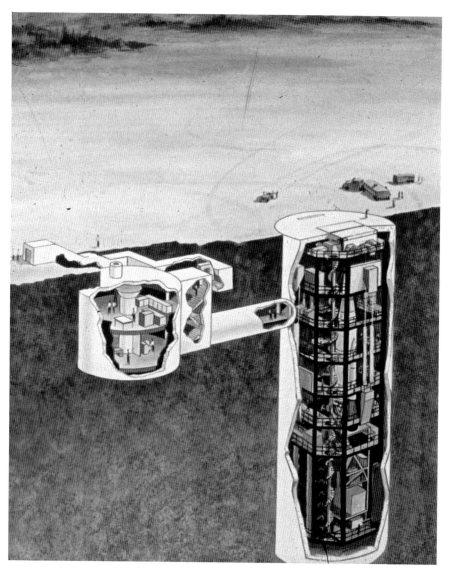

Atlas F missile silo and launch control center (LCC) drawing. *Courtesy of www.atlasmissilesilo.com.*

the Atlas F...facility construction programs," which was done "through a network of CEBMCO area offices, one of which was located at each major site" and oversaw construction.[30] The Schilling AFB Atlas missile sites were initially under the oversight of the Kansas City district of the Army Corps of Engineers until CEBMCO assumed control of the project. Construction

Manitou, Oklahoma Atlas F missile, June 30, 1962. Twelve sites near Schilling Air Force Base in Salina housed Atlas F ICBMs identical to this missile. *Courtesy of www.siloworld.net.*

costs for building ICBM sites was enormous. The United States had spent $2 billion building sites by 1962 and would spend billions more.

The missiles at the Schilling AFB Atlas F sites, along with those at Lincoln AFB in Nebraska, Altus AFB in Oklahoma, Dyess AFB in Texas, Walker AFB in New Mexico and Plattsburg AFB in New York, were the nation's first to be maintained entirely underground in large, protective silos. Each air force base had twelve missile sites attached to it, and they were usually spaced less than forty miles from each other. While the horizontal Atlas E complexes could withstand overpressures of 25 psi, the large vertical Atlas F silos were built to withstand overpressures reaching 100 psi. Lonnquest and Winkler provide this explanation of *overpressure*:

> *The normal atmospheric pressure at sea level is 15 psi. Overpressure is an additional, transient pressure created by the shock or blast wave following a powerful explosion. Buildings collapse at 6 psi overpressure. Humans can withstand up to 30 psi overpressure, but a level over 5 psi can rupture eardrums and cause internal hemorrhaging.*[31]

The May 13, 1959 edition of the *Salina Journal* ran a front-page story announcing that nine sites had been chosen to operate Atlas F missiles within 53 miles of Salina and Schilling Air Force Base. The early cost forecast for the nine sites was $135 million. The story described each launch site as "a virtually independent unit with two main buildings. One, 125 by 125 feet, will store the liquid oxygen fuel that propels the missile." Another building, "with 5,000 square feet, will house alert personnel, control equipment, power generators and other facilities." The newspaper informed its readers that the "Atlas missiles will be part of the striking power of the Strategic Air Command."[32]

Though nine Atlas F sites were originally scheduled to ring Schilling Air Force Base, three were added to the list. Each site was numbered, and the twelve sites were referenced accordingly: Site 1 was at Bennington; Site 2, Abilene; Site 3, Chapman; Site 4, Carlton; Site 5, McPherson; Site 6, Mitchell; Site 7, Kanopolis; Site 8, Wilson; Site 9, Beverly; Site 10, Tescott; Site 11, Glasco; Site 12, Minneapolis. With a $17.2 million bid, Utah-Manhattan-Sundt won the contract for the nine original silos and then won the contract for the additional three silos with another $6.2 million bid. Though the combined bid for all twelve launch sites was $23.4 million, because of changes, unexpectedly precise government standards and excavation problems caused by water levels at multiple sites, that figure eventually doubled.[33]

Each silo required extensive digging. Once the silo was dug, its walls would be created to house the missile and the multistory steel structure that would surround it and allow it to be serviced. Then the vertical steel crib, fifteen stories tall, was built inside the silo to surround the missile and provide space to store its peripheral equipment necessary for maintenance and operation.[34]

Though many people who lived near the missile sites were happy to find jobs constructing them, and states enjoyed the millions of dollars that their construction pumped into their economies, some local residents were unhappy with the missile sites' arrival. Realizing that nearby missile sites would likely be targets of Soviet nuclear-armed missiles in the event of war, some individuals and groups in Kansas protested at sites under construction. A group of protesting students from McPherson College reportedly damaged an Atlas E site under construction. The municipal government of Roswell received ten fallout shelter building permit requests in October 1961. Kansans' fears were illustrated in a June 19, 1961 *Kansas City Star* cartoon. Captioned "Grim Crop for the Midlands," the cartoon depicted twelve Atlas missiles standing in wheat fields, with pigs rooting around near missiles in the foreground and a farmhouse just behind the dozen missiles in the background.[35]

The Friday, May 6, 1960 edition of the *Salina Journal* carried a front-page story about several McPherson College students and others protesting the Atlas F site nearby. These students adopted a "love and peace" mantra and posted protest signs with slogans, including "Love, Not Missiles," and "Love Is the Weapon for Peace," beside U.S. Highway 81 less than two miles from the Atlas complex near a site access road that was under construction. Paul H. Stern, a twenty-nine-year-old ministerial student who was married and had one child, was one of the protest group's three leaders. Stern emphasized that the protesters were not acting on behalf of the college. He also clarified that Schilling Air Force Base was not the specific target of the protest; rather, the students were protesting worldwide nuclear armaments and hoped to effect global peace.[36]

American pilot Francis Gary Powers flew a U-2 spy plane that was shot down while flying a reconnaissance mission over the Soviet Union on May 1, 1960. Two days after informing its readers of the McPherson site protests, the *Salina Journal* published an Associated Press story on its front page conveying that Soviet leader Nikita Khrushchev reported that Powers had admitted to committing espionage on behalf of the United States. Khrushchev shared some items that had been taken from Powers as evidence that the American was in Soviet custody, and he also said that Powers would be put on trial. The story said that "Khrushchev waved pictures before a shouting, applauding Parliament—the Supreme Soviet—in support of his charge that the 30-year-old pilot was photographing

Soviet military bases and industrial installations for the U.S. Central Intelligence Agency."[37]

Three weeks later, the final three Schilling-area Atlas F sites to be added to the original nine were formally announced. The May 29, 1960 edition of the *Salina Journal* described Site 10 as being located "Three miles north of Minneapolis on the east side of US81 Highway"; Site 11 as "Three miles northwest of Abilene"; and Site 12 as "1½ miles east of Tescott on the north side of K-18 highway." Excavation at the Wilson and Chapman sites was scheduled to begin the following week.[38]

Evidenced by the two Forbes-area construction fatalities, building ICBM launch sites was dangerous; nationally, more than fifty people died in silo accidents.[39] The Schilling AFB sites were not immune from the danger; five men died during site construction. The Salina newspaper reported the July 23, 1960 death of Merle Jennings, a middle-aged carpenter from Ozark, Missouri. Jennings was on the job at the Carlton Atlas site, when a wooden form weighing hundreds of pounds used for shaping poured concrete to create silo walls dropped from forty feet overhead and fell on Jennings's head. The Salina newspaper described the process of creating walls for each silo near Schilling Air Force Base: "The circular concrete wall is being poured as a single unit. Forms are inched upward as the concrete dries." According to the story, Jennings was at the silo floor when he was struck by the heavy form that fell as it was being raised.[40]

In the midst of building Atlas F missile sites, Kansas politics continued as usual. Primary voters went to the polls on August 2, 1960, and the following day, the *Salina Journal* reported that Republican lawyer Robert Dole, thirty-seven, of Russell, had provisionally beaten Keith Sebelius by about six hundred votes in a race for the state's Sixth Congressional seat. The Associated Press listed Dole's lead as slightly greater than six hundred votes. The story relayed that if his lead held, Dole would face William A. Davis, a farmer from Goodland, in the general election for the congressional seat.[41]

The same day that Dole's provisional victory over Sebelius in the Kansas Sixth Congressional District primary was reported, Alvin Leikam, twenty, from Hays, became the second Schilling-area fatality during Atlas F site construction. On Wednesday, August 3, 1960, the truck loaded with concrete that Leikam was driving from the Minneapolis site to the Wilson site ran off the road into a ditch, rolled and caught fire.[42]

Barely more than two months later, twenty-year-old J.C. Nelson became the third site-related death when he fell about 165 feet to the bottom of the Minneapolis silo.[43] The following month, tragedy struck at the Glasco Atlas missile site when twenty-six-year-old steel worker James E. Mills of Tulsa, Oklahoma, died after falling more than 150 feet inside the silo there.[44]

The fifth and final Schilling-area site fatality was twenty-five-year-old David Moody of Chapman. The *Salina Journal* reported that the January 6, 1961 incident occurred because a heavy pipe fell more than thirty feet and struck Moody, "an engineering aide for Wilson and Company," as he worked inside the silo, causing him to fall twenty-five feet to the silo floor. Moody, who had lived in Salina more than four years, left behind a widow and two children, ages four and three.[45]

In addition to fatalities, constructing the Schilling Atlas sites resulted in several nonfatal accidents, including fifteen falls; eleven injuries causing strains, sprains, bruises and cuts; five incidents of falling objects striking workers; and four burns. Though weather problems were not extreme, traveling to and from the sites in winter could be difficult, because, as the official Corps of Engineers history of the Schilling sites noted, "when it snows in Kansas—IT SNOWS."[46]

When President John F. Kennedy entered the White House in January 1961, he was determined to change national defense policy. During the 1960 presidential campaign, Kennedy had been critical of the Eisenhower administration's Massive Retaliation approach, and upon assuming office, he implemented a "Flexible Response" policy, allowing for a range of military options against enemy aggression that included nonnuclear actions.[47] Kennedy continued to expand the nation's nuclear capabilities, though. In President Eisenhower's final year in office in 1960, the United States had twelve ICBMs and approximately 1,500 long-range bombers.[48] In March 1961, President Kennedy wanted to expand the defense budget to increase the stockpile of ICBMs, the number of Polaris submarines that carried nuclear missiles aimed at the Soviet Union and the number of B-52 bombers on constant alert.[49] Two months later, in a special message to Congress, President Kennedy spoke of the need to maintain a nuclear arsenal of such overwhelming force that no nation would dare to threaten us to use it: "We will deter an enemy from making a nuclear attack only if our retaliatory power is so strong and so invulnerable that he knows he would be destroyed by our response."[50]

Kansas coverage of the disastrous April 1961 Bay of Pigs Invasion included multiple front-page stories in the April 17 edition of the *Salina Journal*. "Cuba Invaded: Liberation Fight Opens" and "Russia Threatens to Give Military Help to Castro" were the headlines of two stories informing Kansans that American-backed Cuban exiles had washed ashore in Cuba to remove the Communist leader Fidel Castro from power, and the Soviet Union was promising to supply its Cuban comrades with "all the necessary assistance." U.S. senator Kenneth Keating, a New York Republican, warned that if Soviet premier Nikita Khrushchev attempted to intervene in Cuba, the country should "block him by any appropriate and effective means" and that introduction of Soviet personnel there would obligate the United States to implement a naval blockade to avoid the introduction of Soviet troops. This crisis presaged another, more dangerous, Cuban crisis eighteen months later that would involve Soviet nuclear missiles and in which the Forbes-area missiles and Schilling-area missiles would play a prominent role, as would several missiles located near Wichita's McConnell Air Force Base.[51]

Two months after the Bay of Pigs incident, the twelve Schilling-area Atlas missile sites were turned over to the air force. The event was marked during a June 16, 1961 ceremony at the Chapman site in which the Utah-Manhattan-Sundt Construction Company formally presented the sites to the air force. Though initial construction was completed, machinery and the missiles themselves remained to be installed at the sites under the oversight of the Air Force Site Activation Task Force. Ultimately, the bases would be handed to the Strategic Air Command.[52]

The Utah-Manhattan-Sundt construction manager of the Schilling-area silo construction called the project the most difficult one he had worked on in his many years on the job. The steel springs supporting the cribs inside those twelve silos were the heaviest in the world. A multitude of small equipment pieces had to be devised and installed in an absolutely clean environment. Two large diesel-powered generators provided electricity to run equipment. Site visitors attending the Chapman ceremony viewed the silo and launch control center and saw for themselves the expansive underground nuclear weapon storage and operations facility. Air Force Site Activation Task Force commander Colonel Arthur W. Cruikshank spoke during the event and said that he hoped the missiles succeeded in preventing a Soviet nuclear attack: "I don't know how long they'll be needed, but I hope Atlas missiles in the fields outside Salina will serve their purpose [of deterring war] without ever having to be fired in anger."[53]

Along with the news that the initial construction of the twelve Atlas F missile launch complexes was complete, Henry B. Jameson, editor and general manager of the *Abilene Daily Reflector-Chronicle*, theorized that Abilene would be targeted by the Soviet Union if war came. On June 17, he wrote:

> *This is not intended as a "scare" story. But it would be foolhardy for us to pretend there is nothing to fear like the ostrich sticking its head in the sand, or the proverbial optimist who looked the other way hoping the problem would go away. If this country ever becomes involved in a nuclear war Abilene and this entire central Kansas area will be smack in a prime enemy target area.*[54]

Jameson reported that this conclusion was based on information that he had gotten from military personnel, including "some of the nation's top missile experts," during ceremonies marking the completion of initial Schilling AFB missile-site construction and their being turned over to the military.

Because Jameson toured the site northwest of Chapman, he gave a firsthand description to his readers:

> *The silo portion is divided into eight levels and under these is still enough room to place a three story building. Each level, all around the center circle which will hold the missile, is crammed with complicated equipment or prepared to receive it in the next phase of work. Huge diesels generate power for lights, air conditioning and scores of other uses. Winding steel steps lead from one level to the other—but there is also a large elevator which is busy most of the time.*

He went on to inform his readers that the United States was capable, if necessary, of firing seventy-two Atlas F missiles in fifteen minutes, in concert or succession, virtually anywhere on earth, and that they would arrive quickly and within two nautical miles of their targets, having traveled thousands of miles an hour. To convey the enormous size of each Atlas missile silo, Jameson relayed that all the sites silos combined "could hold five million more bushels than the total grain elevator capacity of the city of Indianapolis." In addition, Jameson continued, "the concrete in them would build a highway 20 feet wide and six inches thick from St. Louis past Chicago."[55]

Shortly after the Schilling-area Atlas missile sites were turned over to the air force, the *Salina Journal* reported the unfolding Berlin Crisis. President Kennedy met with Soviet premier Nikita Khrushchev in Vienna, Austria, earlier in the month, and Khrushchev issued a deadline for the United

States to leave West Berlin—where the United States had maintained a presence since World War II ended in 1945—or face war. Eager to stop the mass exodus each year of hundreds of thousands of East Germans fleeing Communism through Berlin, Khrushchev stopped access from East Berlin into West Berlin August 13, 1961, by erecting the Berlin Wall—first a temporary barbed-wire fence, followed eventually by the permanent stone wall that would divide the city for another twenty-eight years.[56]

The June 23, 1961 edition of the Salina newspaper carried multiple front-page Associated Press stories about the crisis. One conveyed that Secretary of State Dean Rusk reiterated the hard-won rights of the Americans, British and French to be in Berlin and the unwillingness to relinquish those occupation rights. Another declared, "Congress generally agrees that the West faces an early showdown with Soviet Premier Khrushchev over Berlin that could erupt into a third world war." Two days later, the local newspaper carried another front-page Associated Press story declaring that free West Berlin was important because it "lies close to the heart of the Western Alliance which is the mainstay of the U.S. global defense system—and there is little room for the West to yield on this Red-encircled city without giving it all to the Communists."[57] The story also warned that a small fight over Berlin could dramatically and promptly escalate since both nations possessed nuclear weapons.

American ICBM sites were assumed to be targeted in the event of a Soviet attack, and the October 25, 1961 edition of the *Salina Journal* carried an Associated Press story speculating that the nation's military bases, including Schilling AFB, would be in the Soviet crosshairs for a nuclear strike. The story referenced a 1960 study conducted "by government meteorologists" of the projected results of an attack on American ICBM locations. According to the study, an attack would mean a 50 percent chance that fallout would be a problem for Schilling Air Force Base and the city of Salina.[58] Evidencing local concern, a story in the Salina newspaper the previous week announced that a public information session on surviving an atomic attack would be held Thursday, October 18 at Schilling AFB in the base theater.[59]

Further heightening fears was news that the Soviet Union detonated the most powerful nuclear weapon in history. Two weeks before the October 29, 1961 explosion of a fifty-megaton Soviet nuclear bomb, Soviet leader Nikita Khrushchev announced that his nation would complete nuclear testing by detonating what was called a "superbomb." The metaphorical fallout included a spirited debate between American ambassador to the

United Nations Adlai Stevenson and his Soviet counterpart, Semyon K. Tsarapkin. Stevenson "accused the Soviet Union of pushing the world toward disaster,"[60] and Tsarapkin responded that the Soviet Union was merely trying to deter the United States from starting nuclear conflict. The most powerful American nuclear weapon that had been detonated at that point did not exceed twenty megatons.

The Schilling-area Atlas missile sites were transferred to Strategic Air Command in a ceremony on September 13, 1962, at the Carneiro site. Schilling's 22nd Strategic Aerospace Division commander Colonel Jack W. Hayes Jr. assumed control of the sites on behalf of the air force. The event included a display of the site's Atlas missile, described by the local newspaper in these words: "As the ceremony began, buttons were pushed and the massive missile's silvery snout poked up from its cavern. In slow splendor, the missile reared upward on its elevator until its full length loomed against the blue sky, an awesome symbol of America's might." Several individuals were recognized for distinction at the ceremony. Paul S. Gordon, the Carneiro site supervisor, received a commendation for finishing that site's silo while using a fourth fewer workers than all other sites. Additionally, A.J. Galey, launch complex chief, received a commendation, as did Clem Bangers, president of the Salina Building Trades Council. As many as 3,200 individuals worked on the sites while under construction.[61]

In mid-October 1962, only one month after Kansas's twelve Atlas F missile sites became the property of the U.S. Air Force, the nation—and the world—entered into the most dangerous two weeks of the Cold War. The Kennedy administration learned that the Soviet Union was building sites in Cuba capable of launching nuclear missiles against the United States, and the Cuban Missile Crisis began. Because of the crisis, all twelve missiles assigned to the 550th Strategic Missile Squadron at Schilling Air Force Base were put on alert.[62] President Kennedy made a televised address the evening of October 22 and informed the nation about the Soviet imposition of missile bases in Cuba and that he was ordering a naval blockade—called a "quarantine"—there to prevent further offensive Soviet weaponry from reaching the island nation.[63]

As President Kennedy planned the strategy to counter Soviet moves a mere ninety miles from the United States, Schilling Air Force Base was placed on alert. The October 23, 1962 edition of the *Salina Journal* ran a front-page story announcing that Schilling Air Force Base had been put on alert but reported that the base refused to confirm that this was a result of the Cuba situation. In fact, Schilling AFB's information officer claimed that

Left: Atlas F missile on front page of *Salina Journal*, September 13, 1962. *Courtesy of www. siloworld.net.*

Right: Atlas F missile and silo door in *Salina Journal*, September 13, 1962. *Courtesy of www. siloworld.net.*

the base was occasionally placed on alert, and this was nothing out of the ordinary. However, base officials refused to comment on the Cuban crisis to the newspaper. The newspaper did report that "some planes and men had been shifted elsewhere."[64]

Fortunately, the Cuban crisis ended peacefully, and none of Kansas's intercontinental ballistic missiles was fired toward a Communist enemy, nor would they ever be. Within three years, the Schilling-area missiles would leave Kansas. Between June 1, 1963, and March 9, 1964, three Atlas F sites attached to Walker Air Force Base in New Mexico were destroyed during propellant loading exercises. On May 14, 1964, an Atlas F site attached to Altus Air Force Base in Oklahoma was also destroyed by an explosion during a propellant load exercise. Two days after the Oklahoma explosion, Secretary McNamara announced that the Atlas E series would be phased out by the end of fiscal year 1965.[65] Because the first-generation American ICBMs were considered obsolete, in November 1964 Secretary McNamara announced that all—including the Atlas E and F and Titan I—would be retired the following year. The 548th Strategic Missile Squadron at Forbes AFB was officially deactivated on March 25, 1965. Between January and March 1965, Strategic Air Command removed all Atlas F missiles and shipped them to Norton Air Force Base at San Bernardino, California, for storage.[66]

Every Atlas ICBM had thousands of parts, and occasionally each was required to be removed from operational status and transported to the missile assembly building, or MAB, for routine maintenance. Each air force base that operated an ICBM squadron included a MAB. Salinans were informed during the first week of January 1965 that the first Atlas F missile from Schilling Air Force Base had been shipped to Norton AFB the previous week. The local newspaper described that missile as "the replacement spare in Schilling's 12 launching missile complexes" that "had been kept in the missile assembly and maintenance shop at Schilling." The missiles at the twelve sites near Salina remained on alert, and though their actual date of removal was still classified in January, they were on schedule to be deactivated by the end of June, followed by Schilling AFB's closure. The entire Atlas program was being phased out in favor of more modern quick-launching Minuteman and Titan II ICBMs. The General Services Agency put the Atlas E and F and Titan I sites up for sale and even ran an ad in an April 1965 edition of the *Wall Street Journal* that listed the Forbes AFB and Schilling AFB sites.[67]

As the clock ran out on the Atlas program in Kansas, the air force crew that operated each missile was downsized from five men to three. Because of flooding in June 1965, the Carlton Atlas F crew of Staff Sergeant Kenneth Eilts, Airman First Class Richard Harmon and Airman Third Class David Siferd had its tour of duty slightly extended. The Salina newspaper described the site as being "on a hill a few miles inside the Dickinson county line, southeast of Gypsum and near Carlton." Though the Carlton site crew members' twenty-four hours on duty should have ended at 9:00 a.m., Saturday, June 26, they had to remain at the site because the replacement crew had to stop at Gypsum, unable to continue on to Carlton because of high waters. Instead, the air force called the Carlton Co-op elevator manager, who sent some locals to the site, and they took Eilts to a grocery store to purchase enough food to sustain them until they could leave the site.[68]

The U.S. government chose to sell the surplus Kansas Atlas sites, and it was already soliciting bids on equipment before the end of 1965.

On November 31, bids were unsealed from fifteen different groups and individuals who wanted to buy equipment. With its bid of $76,789.99, Lesco Automotive Corporation of Brooklyn, New York, was the high bidder. Contingent on winning a contract was the willingness to help the federal government remove any salvageable equipment from a missile site. Bidders competed for silo equipment that included "elevator drive systems, which raised and lowered the missiles, heavy duty hydraulic pumping systems, vacuum type tanks for storing liquid oxygen and nitrogen, plastic-lined steel tanks for storing rocket fuel, regulating and filtering equipment and some 550 tons of structural steel," reported the *Salina Journal* on December 1. The seven Kansas bidders were "Tucker Construction Co. and Central Wrecking and Construction Inc. of Wichita; Wholesale Lumber Inc. of Salina; M.F. English Construction Co. of Hutchinson; Robins Construction Co. of Minneapolis; Wallace D. McPherson and a bidder identified only as Howick, both of Topeka."[69]

TITAN

While work was underway readying the Atlas missile for operation in the 1950s, in 1955 the air force began developing another liquid-fueled ICBM, the Titan I, as an insurance policy in case of Atlas failure. The Titan was developed by the Martin Company, which, along with related contractors, employed sixteen thousand people who worked on the missile by September 1958. As the Titan was being developed, the Army Corps of Engineers oversaw the Titan I launch sites, which were larger and costlier than any other ICBM launch complexes. Like the Atlas F, the Titan was stored in hardened underground silos built to withstand overpressures of one hundred psi. To survive a nuclear attack and remain operational to launch a retaliatory strike, "the missile silos, control center, powerhouse, and various other support facilities were connected by almost half a mile of steel tunnel, all buried more than 40 feet underground."[70] Also like the Atlas F, the Titan I would be fueled within the silo, raised by an elevator through the open silo doors until completely above the ground surface and then fired.

In 1959, the air force began developing the larger Titan II. The Titan I was 98 feet long and 10 feet wide, and the Titan II, the nation's largest ever ICBM, was 108 feet long and 10 feet wide. The Titan I's range was

6,300 miles, whereas the Titan II could fly up to 9,000 miles. In addition to the Titan II being the largest ICBM, it also has the distinction of having carried the most powerful nuclear warhead of any missile. Whereas the Titan I carried a 4-megaton warhead, the Titan II's 9-megaton warhead was more than twice as powerful. According to the United States National Park Service, each Titan II warhead contained "three times the explosive power of all the bombs used during World War II, including both atomic bombs." Another important advantage that the Titan II had was launch time. Since its liquid fuel was stored outside the missile, Titan I launch required about 15 minutes. The Titan II's liquid fuel and oxidizer were stored inside the missile, which allowed the Titan II to be fired from inside the silo in only one minute. Missile maintenance was also easier, and the risk of accidents was reduced.[71]

Only three air force bases operated the massive and extremely powerful Titan II missile launch sites: Davis-Monthan Air Force Base in Arizona, Little Rock Air Force Base in Arkansas and McConnell Air Force Base near Wichita. McConnell AFB was chosen as the hub for eighteen Titan II missiles silos, operated by the 532nd Strategic Missile Squadron and the 533rd Strategic Missile Squadron, attached to the 381st Strategic Missile Wing at McConnell. Eighteen silos were built, creating what has been called a rough horseshoe around Wichita. Titan II launch sites attached to the 532nd SMS included one each at Conway Springs, Kingman, Mount Vernon, Murdock, Norwich, Rago and Viola and two at Wellington. The 533rd SMS operated three Titan II sites at Leon and one each at El Dorado, Oxford, Potwin, Rock, Smileyville and Winfield.[72]

Titan IIs were distributed so that each squadron included nine launch sites. In all, six Titan II squadrons were deployed by the air force, and to cut costs, "squadrons were grouped in pairs, forming an operational base."[73] Each Titan II silo was 147 feet deep with a 55-foot diameter and was constructed with fortified concrete. The silo interior included nine separate levels with space to operate equipment and access the missile. Each silo included a 740-ton door made of concrete and steel that could open in about 20 seconds. A tunnel 250 feet long connected each Titan II silo to its launch control center. Between the two, however, was a heavily reinforced concrete building called the blast lock. The four-person air force crews entered the three-level dome-shaped reinforced-concrete launch control room 37 feet in diameter—that included all of the equipment necessary to launch the missile, communication equipment, a kitchen area and a sleeping area—through a 35-foot-deep passageway

Titan II missile in silo. *Courtesy of www. wikimedia.org.*

that began at the surface and ended at the blast lock. Both blast lock ends were covered by 6,000-pound steel blast doors built to protect the launch control center from either a nuclear explosion at the surface or the Titan II exploding inside the silo. The doors were reinforced to protect against an overpressure of 1,000 psi.

The McConnell-area missile sites employed three phases for construction at those locations. The Fuller-Webb-Hardeman construction firms won the contract in December 1960 for the first phase with their approximately $30.8 million joint bid. Phase I for the McConnell sites was completed on February 21, 1962. The Phase II construction contract was won by Martin K. Eby Incorporated and Associates in June 1961, with a $37.6 million bid. Work began on December 4, 1961, and was completed a year later. The third phase found the Martin Company as the Site Activation Task Force working together to finalize the silos in order to turn them over the Strategic Air Command. In all, 2,200 people, including many who had worked at the Kansas Atlas E and F sites, worked on the $68.4 million Titan II sites while they were under construction. The air force assumed control of the final McConnell-area Titan II silo on January 31, 1963.[74]

ONE FATALITY OCCURRED DURING construction of the McConnell AFB missile sites. Then, on August 24, 1978, two air force personnel, Staff Sergeant Robert J. Thomas and Airman First Class Erby Hepstall, died resulting from a fuel oxidizer leak at the Rock missile site. Nearby residents were evacuated as a precaution, and the site sustained damage. Deputy Secretary of Defense Frank Carlucci ordered that the Titan II program be inactivated on October 2, 1981. The first McConnell-area launch site that was changed from alert status was Launch Complex 533-8 at Winfield. The process was completed, and all McConnell sites were deactivated by August 8, 1986.[75]

NIKE

The Soviet acquisition of atomic weapons in 1949 forced the United States to prepare to defend against a Soviet atomic attack by airplane. A reevaluation of American foreign and defense policy occasioned by multiple events, including the American loss of its atomic monopoly to the Soviets, resulted in a 1950 document known as NSC 68. The paper stated that the Soviet Union would have a large stockpile of atomic bombs and the ability to deliver them inside the United States by 1954, requiring dramatic increases in defense spending. To strengthen its defensive capabilities against such a Soviet long-range bomber attack, the United States sped up its work on the Nike surface-to-air missile. The U.S. Army began developing the Nike Ajax antiaircraft missile in 1945, with deployment of the first Nike battery in 1954. The liquid-fueled Ajax was 34 feet long, had a 30-mile range, could operate at an altitude of 70,000 feet and carried a conventional bomb. In 1958, 200 Nike batteries were scattered across the nation. The same year, the army deployed the newer Nike Hercules as it began phasing out the Ajax. The solid-fueled Hercules was 41 feet long, had a 75-mile range and was operational at an altitude of up to 150,000 feet. The first among antiaircraft missiles to carry a nuclear warhead, the Nike Hercules was deployed at 137 locations.[76]

Whereas America's ICBMs were housed in rural locations, the Nike launch sites were near the nation's large cities and surrounding metropolitan areas. The sites, built beginning in the late 1950s, stood only one story, were made of cinderblocks and reportedly resembled the many school buildings built to accommodate baby boom children who filled schools during the decade. By 1958, just five years after the army received permission to develop a second-generation surface-to-air missile, the Nike Hercules was ready for deployment near New York, Chicago and Philadelphia. In the late 1950s and early '60s, the Hercules was positioned close to cities that included St. Louis and Kansas City as well as near several Strategic Air Command bases.[77]

Two Nike Hercules batteries, designated KC-60 and KC-80, were placed in Kansas, and two more were placed in Missouri in 1960 to defend Kansas City because of its importance as both a transportation center and as an industrial center. One Kansas Hercules site was near Gardner and the other was at Fort Leavenworth. A highly publicized groundbreaking ceremony that included Kansas governor George Docking was held for the Leavenworth site. The Kansas City District of the Army Corps of Engineers supervised site construction. Though cost for all of the sites was estimated to be $6 million, needed modifications increased final costs. Headquarters and a command and control were located at Olathe Naval Air Station. Although two Hercules batteries were scheduled to be placed at Schilling Air Force Base to protect the Salina-area Atlas F ICBM launch sites, the Department of Defense canceled the project after construction had begun. In fact, a Schilling headquarters operated at Bennington for two months from April to June 1960. The four Kansas City–area sites were operational between 1960 and 1969. As the bomber threat was overtaken by the Soviet ICBM threat, all remaining Nike Hercules batteries were deactivated by 1974.[78]

The Missouri locations for the Nike Hercules batteries assigned to protect Kansas City were Lawson and Pleasant Hill. For the Gardner, Kansas site, agricultural land south of town owned by Alonzo L. Harlan and Walter Fajen was bought for the Nike Missile Base, which opened in October 1959. Base commanding officer was Lieutenant Colonel Ralph Miller. German Shepherds guarded all four of the Nike bases protecting Kansas City. The Gardner launch site operated thirteen Nike Hercules missiles in three magazines. According to a 2015 story in the *Gardner News*, the base headquarters, north of 199th Street and Gardner Road, included a "PX, a men's club, and a barbershop."[79] The commanding officer who oversaw base closure in February 1969 was Second Lieutenant Dale Nichols.

Left: Photo of Nike Hercules missile ready for launch displayed on program for July 23, 1958 Fort Leavenworth groundbreaking ceremony. *U.S. Army photo courtesy of Fort Leavenworth Garrison Public Affairs Office.*

Right; Mock Nike Hercules missile atop Administration Area of Battery D, 5th Missile Battalion, 55th Artillery, known as Nez Perce Village today. *U.S. Army photo courtesy of Fort Leavenworth Garrison Public Affairs Office.*

The Leavenworth Nike site was formally known as Site KC-80, and according to the *Ft. Leavenworth Lamp*, it "was the home of Battery D, 5th Missile Battalion, 55th Artillery. The battery complex occupied several locations around Fort Leavenworth—a headquarters and administration area, an integrated fire control and radar site, a magazine and launch facility and an assembly and maintenance building." Work began on the flat-roofed cinderblock buildings in July 1958. The Leavenworth site was activated by November 1959, though the final building was completed two years later. Just under a decade later, in February 1969, the Leavenworth Nike battery was inactivated, and all site locations were decommissioned. The *Lamp* provided this site description:

> *The fire control site with its array of missile tracking, target tracking and target ranging radars was on Government Hill, the high ground north of the Hancock Gate. The launch site with its underground magazines*

and above ground erector/launchers was on the flat area along Sheridan Drive overlooking Salt Creek Valley in an area once called Bell Point. The ready magazine for special weapons was in an undisclosed location. The headquarters area—with orderly room, supply room, barracks and other administration support structures—was where Lowe Avenue and Nez Perce Village now sit. The missile assembly building was near the airfield so it could receive missiles, supplies and equipment by air or rail. Operational for more than nine years, it never fired a shot.[80]

As the U.S. Air Force characterized it, the advent of the ICBM force in 1960 ushered in an "uneasy half-peace" between the United States and the Soviet Union. Though conflicts arose, nuclear war did not. According to Jacob Neufeld in *The Development of Ballistic Missiles in the United States Air Force 1945–1960*, both sides enhanced their stockpiles of ICBMs "over the years to ensure their ability to inflict 'unacceptable damage' upon the enemy under any conditions." Possession of possibly civilization-altering weapons gave both sides pause. As Neufeld put it, ICBMs were "a paradox—thousands of them waiting to unleash total destruction, but the very fact of their presence ensuring their non-use."[81]

The Kennedy administration operated with the hope that the Soviet Union would not initiate a nuclear war knowing that both countries would be destroyed. This was the essence of the doctrine of "mutual assured destruction," or MAD.[82] Signaling his agreement with this philosophy, during the October 1962 Cuban Missile Crisis, Soviet leader Nikita Khrushchev pleaded with President Kennedy by letter to join him in taking the necessary steps to avoid the "catastrophe of thermonuclear war" between the two countries: "Only lunatics or suicides, who themselves want to perish and to destroy the whole world before they die, could" allow such a war to happen.[83] During the crisis, one of Secretary of Defense Robert McNamara's aides explained that 841 American nuclear weapons would survive a Soviet first strike against the United States that did not include the Cuban missiles, and even a Soviet first strike that included the Cuban missiles would leave the United States with more than 480 nuclear weapons with which to retaliate—including most of the hardened underground missile sites—and inflict much greater damage on the Soviet Union than had been inflicted on the United States. In October 1962, the United States possessed 240 long-range missiles capable of reaching the Soviet Union—144 ICBMs and 96 missiles aboard Polaris submarines.[84] Nikita Khrushchev was keenly aware of the American nuclear arsenal's destructive capability, which moved him to implore President Kennedy to join him in avoiding nuclear war. That arsenal included nine Atlas E intercontinental ballistic missiles near Forbes Air Force Base, twelve Atlas F ICBMs near Schilling Air Force Base and eighteen Titan II ICBMs near McConnell Air Force Base.

The Atlas E and F missile sites in Kansas were operational for only a few years, and they were extremely costly—both in terms of money and the seven lives lost—to build and operate, as were the Titan II missiles that were operational much longer. Millions were also spent building state Nike missile sites. As an integral part of a national security priority that spanned presidencies from Eisenhower in the 1950s to Reagan in the 1980s, little monetary expense was spared in program development and site construction. Businesses reaped the benefits of constructing those missile sites, and thousands of Kansans and others benefitted from site-related job opportunities as Kansans learned to live with nuclear weapons in their midst as part of daily life. The state benefitted economically, but the nation benefitted from Kansas's missiles because they defended Americans against possible attack and strengthened the American nuclear arsenal that deterred Soviet aggression and saved the nation from catastrophe.

3

AFTER THE OBSOLESCENCE

The U.S. government began divesting itself of missile-site properties when the Atlas, Titan and Nike programs were decommissioned. Some properties were sold to private owners, some to public school districts and some to a Kansas university. Their various uses have been domestic, profitable and educational.

Kansas State University acquired three former Atlas missile sites on September 30, 1966. In formal ceremonies in Manhattan, the U.S. Air Force transferred ownership of two Atlas F sites and one Atlas E site to university president James A. McCain. Attending the ceremony were air force personnel from Schilling Air Force Base and Forbes Air Force Base, representatives from the Kansas Board of Regents, federal and state government officials and Kansas State University College of Engineering faculty members. According to the November 1966 edition of the Kansas State College of Engineering newsletter, the Atlas E site near Wamego was the first to receive transfer approval: "The site, which is virtually intact except for the missile and associated electronic components, will be converted to a unique aerospace laboratory by the College of Engineering." The two Atlas F sites were at Abilene and Chapman. The sites were valuable because they provided research and instructional facilities that could not be provided on campus for engineering students where rockets engines would be utilized and high-voltage electricity and highly pressurized water would be needed. Additionally, the former missile sites were ideal, because they provided communications via telephone as well as protection from extreme

Kansas weather and vandalism. Recognizing their value, when Dr. James Bowyer with the university's mechanical engineering department learned that the Forbes AFB Atlas E program would be deactivated and the sites would become available, he decided to pursue the Wamego site. According to the department newsletter, the site "was sufficiently remote that noise could be tolerated and personnel, fire protection and utilities were available, and much of the auxiliary equipment and other test facilities needed for a modern space laboratory were also included in the missile launch sites." The university submitted a formal request to the General Services Administration, which led to the university's acquisition of the missile sites.[85]

The Wamego site formally became the Mechanical Engineering Department Aerospace Laboratory, where the first departmental experiments were scheduled to take place in "an underground rocket static test facility" and would involve "a $10,000 shock tube facility." The newsletter said that two "small 160-pound thrust rocket engines will be installed in the missile bay and flame tunnel" for experiments. The reinforced concrete used to construct the site would provide adequate protection against the heat and sufficient insulation against noise. The Wamego site was fifteen miles from the Kansas State campus in Manhattan and provided electricity, water, sanitation, air conditioning, "hydraulic and pneumatic control systems…storage and transfer systems for various gases and liquids, combustible fuel vapor and gaseous oxygen detection systems, and safety showers and eye wash lavatories."[86]

Byron W. Jones was a Kansas State University undergraduate studying engineering in 1970 and visited the Wamego laboratory site many times. "I don't know how much research was actually conducted there, but I do know they did run a small rocket engine at one point and also a small supersonic wind tunnel," Jones said in a 2019 interview. He remembered that although the Atlas missile and other valuable equipment had been removed before being turned over to the university, large fuel tanks, high-pressure plumbing equipment and other lesser equipment remained, and the facilities were very much intact.[87]

Jones returned to Manhattan in 1978 as a Kansas State University faculty member in the College of Mechanical Engineering. By then, the Wamego site was in a state of disrepair. "The facility had become more of a liability to the department than an asset," Dr. Jones said. "It was a complex facility and very expensive to maintain and was rapidly deteriorating." No longer fit for conducting research, the former Atlas E missile site was mostly used for storage, though occasionally parts would be removed from the site for other purposes. In fact, Jones's visits to the site as a K-State faculty member were mostly to store items or retrieve items from storage. Because of Wamego's population growth, the missile site property became more valuable as real estate than as a research facility and was sold in the early 1990s at auction.[88]

Because of a chemical cleaner called trichloroethylene—used to clean Atlas missile site fuel lines in Kansas—that got dumped at those locations in the 1960s, the Army Corps of Engineers had to follow up to decontaminate the sites, including at the Holton school near Topeka. Responsibility for site decontamination fell to the Department of Defense and the Corps of Engineers. As of November 2009, decontamination projects at sites near Waverly, Keene, Leavenworth and Gardner had been finalized, and more were underway at McPherson, Carlton, Wamego and Holton's Jackson Heights Junior and Senior High School. When the Atlas E site at Holton was deactivated in the mid-1960s, the federal government sold it to the Holton school district for $1, and the school has been there since. The former missile launch site became classrooms, and after a $675,000 bond allowed thirty thousand square feet of classroom additions, underground remodeling and air conditioning installation, the space is used for storage. As of November 2009, the Army Corps of Engineers had spent $20 million cleaning Kansas's Cold War missile sites and estimated that an additional $130 million of work remained to finish the job. When the school was dedicated in late 1969, it served 154 students from four communities: Circleville, Netawaka, Soldier and Whiting.[89]

Matthew Fulkerson turned an Atlas missile site into an Airbnb, a privately owned residence that may be rented as a brief-stay getaway. The site's owners, Ed and Dianna Peden, began living in the abandoned missile site in 1994 and approved Fulkerson's idea. The Subterra Castle Airbnb opened in 2017 and is located fifteen miles south and west of Topeka in the Dover Atlas E site. According to Fulkerson in a 2017 Associated Press article the *Denver Post*, "In addition to a main-floor bedroom, Airbnb guests at Subterra will have a full kitchen, private bathroom, laundry services and a fireplace which gives a 'nice, cozy feeling in the fall and winter months.'" Subterra Castle near Topeka was the first Airbnb housed in a missile site, and as of its 2017 opening, it was the only one.[90]

A 2019 *Topeka Capital-Journal* story carried in *U.S. News & World Report* credits Fulkerson and his wife, Leigh Ann, with purchasing the Schilling-area Atlas F missile site located at Wilson in 2013. They envisioned its becoming an "'eco-adventure resort,' complete with guest suites, a spa, gym, lounge and pool areas, creative spaces, an educational center, a library and so much more." The Fulkersons said they also intend to turn the silo launch control center into headquarters for Matthew's nonprofit S.T.E.A.M. institute to educate the public. As of August 2019, the missile site was still being renovated, but they were already entertaining guests from as far away as San Francisco and China who wanted the missile-site experience and willingly paid the fifty-nine dollars per night to camp outside the site and tour the silo.[91]

Prompted by the September 11, 2001 terrorist attacks on the United States, Larry Hall bought one of the Kansas Atlas missile sites in 2008 for $300,000 and spent $20 million turning it into a survival condo for deep-pocketed folks who want protection from all manner of catastrophe. Described as "one of the world's most extravagant doomsday shelters," Hall's Kansas condos can house twelve families who want posh protection from calamities ranging from nuclear war to epidemics to natural disasters. To protect the privacy of its occupants, Hall wouldn't identify the site's specific location, saying only that it's "situated north of Wichita, Kansas, surrounded by rolling hills and farmland."[92]

The site's fifteen floors provide space for twelve separate 1,820-square-foot family homes that can house six to ten people, each of which provides three bedrooms, two bathrooms, a kitchen, a dining area and a living room. Each home also includes a clothes washer and dryer and a dishwasher. Residents may also see the aboveground world outside through "windows" that have been filled with LED screens and show a live feed of the surrounding area outside the missile site. Each $3 million unit also comes with internet access, use of a gym, a large swimming pool, a climbing wall and a dark park—all inside the underground missile site. To prepare for catastrophe, five years' worth of food is provided for each person, and survival training for residents is mandatory. Guns and ammunition are also stored in case of emergency, and a shooting range is available to hone shooting skills. Since a high-speed elevator was installed, residents don't have to walk several flights of stairs coming or going.[93]

After the Gardner Nike based closed, the federal government ceded the property to the Gardner-Edgerton-Antioch School District the following December. A gym was built on the property, and base buildings were retooled for a new junior high. Nike Junior High School opened its doors in August 1971. The Nike Junior High mascot was the Missile. The principal was Wes Oyer, and teachers were Minnie Ashmore and Joe McNulty (math), Charles Barnett (social studies), Bill Dymacek and Bob Graves (science), Malcolm Meyer, Carolyn Pickering and Kipp Willnauer (music) and Gene Wilmouth (physical education). Known as Nike Middle School in the early 2000s, facilities were remodeled and became known as Nike Intermediate School. Few military buildings remain after demolition and new construction on campus. In 2006, the Gardner school district sold the property about a mile south that housed the launch equipment.[94]

The Leavenworth Nike base properties were sold, and buildings were demolished. According to a December 15, 2016 story in the *Fort Leavenworth Lamp*, "Building 75, the former maintenance and assembly building on Chief Joseph Loop, today is occupied by the Army Materiel Command's tactical maintenance equipment shop." The launch and magazine area do reveal some Cold War reminders. "Seven buildings still stand on Bell Point occupied by the Rod and Gun Club, American Water Military Services, and the Family and Morale, Welfare and Recreation recreational vehicle storage lot, identified by the prominent antenna of the former Military Affiliated Radio System station." An RV park is located "on top of the magazine/launch area where three magazines and 12 erector/launchers once protected the northwest approaches to the Kansas City metropolitan area in the days half a century ago when the Soviet Mya-4 Bison and Tu-95 Bear strategic bombers were believed to be the primary threats to North America."[95]

NONMILITARY USES HAVE ABOUNDED for the former Kansas missile sites. From private residences and survival condos to public school districts and university use, assorted army facilities and an RV park, some attempted adaptations have been more successful than others. The properties once used to deter a nuclear attack and defend the nation if necessary have changed purposes, but they remain and remind us of their former importance.

4

SUNFLOWER STATE CIVIL DEFENSE

As the Cold War moved into the nuclear age and tensions with the Soviet Union heightened, all Americans, including Kansans, learned to live with the threat of nuclear war. To increase the likelihood of survival if nuclear war came, national, state and local civil defense organizations took steps to protect the public. Civil defense preparedness became part of everyday life across the nation and across the state. Kansas's communities prepared to survive a nuclear attack during the Cold War's most dangerous years.

In light of the Soviet Union's breaking the American atomic monopoly and acquiring an atomic bomb in 1949, Congress passed, and President Truman signed into law, the Federal Civil Defense Act of 1950, creating the Federal Civil Defense Administration. To protect Americans against a Soviet attack, the FCDA envisioned "a three-stage shelter program which would (1) locate existing shelter, (2) upgrade potential shelter, and (3) construct new shelter in deficit areas in the Nation's 'critical target cities' as designated by the FCDA and the Department of Defense."[96]

In the early 1950s, mass evacuation of the nation's cities was the preferred method of civil defense protection against a Soviet atomic attack. According to the Kansas Historical Society, the City of Topeka partnered with Shawnee County in 1951 and formed "a joint Civil Defense (CD) program responsible for coordinating mass evacuation during a nuclear disaster." While cities around the country investigated the feasibility of using underground caves and the like as fallout shelters as the 1950s ended, Shawnee County decided to locate its fallout shelter underneath its new courthouse in Topeka, completed in the early 1960s. Since the courthouse's functioning as the state capitol during a crisis was viewed as critical, CD officials designed it to accommodate "just 130 essential officials, including county commissioners, law enforcement, and military liaisons," but not the general public. The Kansas Historical Society provided this description of the facility:

> Topeka's new CD Emergency Operations Center was equipped with thick blast doors and an escape hatch to ground level. It contained a cafeteria, surgical center, and dormitories with triple-deck bunks. Along with two weeks' supply of food and water, local judges and county commissioners would reside in an air-conditioned facility powered by a 100-kilowatt generator. More significantly, the Operations Center served as a regional response hub directing relief efforts via a vast communications network linked to the Emergency Broadcast System.[97]

To facilitate its directing of post-disaster relief efforts, Topeka's emergency operations center was also equipped with a red civil defense telephone in the bomb shelter two floors beneath the courthouse to allow government officials to communicate with personnel throughout the state and region. According to the state historical society, the facility was reminiscent of the secret underground bomb shelter built in 1957 at West Virginia's Greenbriar Resort for members of Congress to seek shelter during a Soviet nuclear attack. The red-handled civil defense telephone remained in Topeka's Emergency Operations Center for twenty years, though it was only used one time—when a violent tornado struck Topeka in 1966. The phone was donated to the Kansas Historical Society in 2008 and is among the items in the Historical Society's Kansas Museum of History.[98]

Kansas City civil defense officials prepared to evacuate the city in case of a Soviet nuclear attack, and they used an evacuation map detailing both routes for those leaving the city and emergency personnel to follow in rescuing injured citizens. A 1954 *Evacuation Map of Greater Kansas City* shows "a series of concentric devastation zone circles emanating…from the intersection of 16th and McGee streets, once the headquarters of the 205th Medical Battalion of the Missouri National Guard and the likely military target in the city." The map explains that locations beyond twenty miles from that intersection, in both Kansas and Missouri, would likely be "reasonably safe."[99]

In conjunction with state and local CD committees from both Missouri and Kansas, the Kansas City Civil Defense Department executed an evacuation drill simulating a nuclear attack on November 8, 1954. Ahead of the drill, more than 130,000 copies of the Kansas City evacuation map were printed and distributed. Dubbed "Operation Scamper," the drill began at 1:30 p.m. that day with three CD siren blasts, each lasting one minute. This signaled to the two thousand participating Civil Defense personnel and emergency responders who were taking part of the imminence of the fictional attack. Copies of the map were distributed at checkpoints along the designated evacuation routes by drill participants. Another siren blast was heard at 2:15 p.m. indicating that participants should find shelter underground to protect themselves against heat, fire and radiation that would accompany a nuclear attack. At 2:30 p.m., a conventional bomb was detonated beside the Missouri River to simulate a nuclear bomb explosion. Thanks to a stout wind, the mock radioactive material blown into the air traveled northwest. Had the airborne material actually been radioactive, it would have damaged and interfered with help coming from Leavenworth and North Kansas City and the counties of Clay and Platte.[100]

Following the drill, Kansas City CD officials admitted that they had failed to formulate plans to evacuate patients in hospitals or the incarcerated in prisons. For any Kansas Citians caught unprepared in an actual attack, the committee instructed that they "lie down against the nearest wall, cover your face with your arms, and leave the rest to Providence." In spite of the lack of planning for prisoners and hospital patients, the day after the drill, "Civil Defense Director Charles O. Thrasher called Operation Scamper a complete success. Kansas City was ready."[101]

The November 8, 1954 edition of the *Kansas City Times* carried a picture of Thrasher and CD staffers looking over evacuation routes at police headquarters at Twenty-Seventh Street and Van Brunt Boulevard. Another picture that appeared in the same edition showed the Missouri River bomb explosion and included this caption: "A MUSHROOM CLOUD formed in the simulation of an H-bomb blast at Holmes street and the Missouri river at 2:30 o'clock yesterday. Twenty pounds of TNT, 200-feet of detonating primer cord, gasoline jelly and white phosphorus were placed in a 5-foot hole by Ft. Riley, Kas., chemical warfare experts to produce the effect."[102]

The first Office of Civil Defense Planning director was Russell J. Hopley. The Northwestern Bell Telephone of Omaha, Nebraska president was appointed in 1948, and within months, he published the manual *Civil Defense for National Security* to educate the nation's citizens about steps they could take to protect themselves in an atomic war. The federal government manual emphasized evacuating large cities prior to an atomic attack.

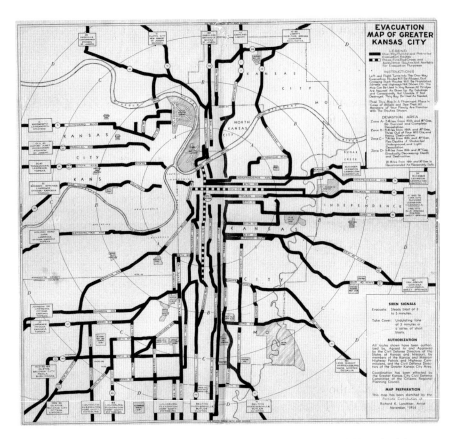

A 1954 Kansas City Civil Defense Evacuation Map. *Courtesy of Missouri Valley Special Collections, Kansas City Public Library, Kansas City, Missouri.*

The "crisis relocation" philosophy was replaced with a shelter-centric approach, and the federal government encouraged Americans to build their own home fallout shelters. CBS television aired a program called *Retrospect*, and an episode in the early 1950s featured the Brown family of Topeka. The Browns, including the two parents and their eight children, were interviewed about the week they spent in their fallout shelter. Their family had an advantage, because the father was a professional builder who constructed the shelter. In fact, the *Encyclopedia of the Great Plains* characterized the episode as less a realistic portrayal of how an American family could survive a nuclear attack than a long commercial for one man's business. The *Encyclopedia* went on to describe such civil defense efforts as "little more than a psychological salve for the American populace" because President Eisenhower's administration realized by the mid-1950s "that nuclear war meant national suicide. Nevertheless, the administration continued to promote the myth of personal responsibility for civil defense in order to avoid demoralizing the American public."[103]

President Eisenhower believed that while the federal government could provide guidance for civil defense, the bulk of those responsibilities lay with state and local governments. However, after learning of the extremely dangerous "blast and thermal effects" of the American hydrogen bomb detonation in 1952, the Soviet Union's hydrogen bomb detonation in 1953 and the "March 1954 BRAVO hydrogen bomb explosion," American policymakers became concerned about the "lethal hazard of long-range radioactive fallout." Many in the American government recognized the danger posed by fallout's spread over thousands of miles after a nuclear explosion, which moved Chet Holifield, chair of the House Military Operations Subcommittee, to scrutinize the Eisenhower administration's civil defense policy. Representative Holifield sponsored H.R. 2125, a bill to elevate civil defense to the cabinet level, emphasizing the primacy of the federal government's civil defense role and establishing "a nationwide shelter system." The FCDA followed suit and proposed a $32 billion national shelter program.[104]

President Eisenhower assigned a committee to study the FCDA shelter plan in April 1957. The Security Resources Panel of the Science Advisory Committee was chaired by H. Rowan Gaither and was known popularly as the "Gaither Committee." The committee made several recommendations to President Eisenhower and the National Security Council, including improving the Strategic Air Command forces, hastening development of intercontinental and intermediate-range ballistic missiles, fortifying intercontinental ballistic missile (ICBM) locations, enlarging American forces and diminishing the vulnerability of American cities. The committee suggested a "passive defense" strategy featuring a $25 billion national program for nuclear fallout shelters to save lives in the event of a nuclear war. Pressure on Eisenhower mounted, caused by two momentous events that year. In August, the Soviet Union launched the first ICBM. Then, in October, the Soviets launched the first artificial satellite, Sputnik, into orbit. Eisenhower responded by merging the FCDA and the Office of Defense Mobilization to create the Office of Civil Defense Mobilization. The administration called on state and local governments to coordinate in creating a national shelter system while merely receiving "advice and guidance" from the federal government.[105]

Eisenhower was loath to spend the huge sums of money necessary for a nationwide shelter program even as policymakers in Washington considered the value of "passive defense" versus "active defense." Delivered to President Eisenhower in November 1957, the Gaither Committee's report, *Deterrence and Survival in the Nuclear Age*, declared that by 1959 the United States would be extremely susceptible to a Soviet ICBM offensive, and it called for a $44 billion increase in defense spending over the next five years, which was "more than the entire defense budget for 1958. Half the money would go for more missiles and bombers…and half for a massive fallout shelter building program and other civil defense."[106]

Though fiscally conservative and wanting to avoid increased spending because of principle, Eisenhower also had another reason to avoid increased defense spending: The U-2 spy plane had provided the president proof that the Soviet Union was not increasing its nuclear arsenal or airplane fleet in preparation for war. Because it was a top- secret program used by the United States to spy on the Soviet Union, Eisenhower did not want to reveal this information or its source, and pressure on Eisenhower to catch up to the Soviet Union mounted. Yet Eisenhower also wanted to avoid giving the false impression to the Soviet government that the United States was preparing for war by building fallout shelters, which could thereby increase the likelihood of war.[107]

Salina participated in a three-day nationwide civil defense drill that began on Tuesday, May 3, 1960. The city's civil defense director, Marie Webb, opened sealed orders and reported, "Evidently, Topeka has been hit," regarding a mock nuclear attack that was part of the drill. Some of the city's schools practiced evacuating buildings in conjunction with the drill. Because participating would have interrupted some students' lunches, the high school did not. Saline County included only two other civil defense directors. Several people from the Saline County Sheriff's Office left to inform schools and CD directors in the area that the drill had begun. The CD director at Gypsum was Alvin Swisher, and the Assaria CD director was Bryce Baily. A story about the drill in the *Salina Journal* conveyed that this test was "the most elaborate test so far of the Conelrad system, which aims to confuse enemy bombers" and explained that "Conelrad stands for control of electronic radiation." Local radio stations changed from normal frequencies to designated 640 and 1240 that Tuesday at noon and carried a recorded statement by President Eisenhower, followed by statements from Secretary of Defense Thomas Gates and national civil defense director Leo Hoegh. The story also reported that, coinciding with the national mock attack drill, "Operation Alert-1960" began, meaning that "key government officials will leave Washington for outlying areas and practice running the government for two days under emergency conditions."[108]

In 1961, Topeka pediatrician Dr. Robert Parman built a fallout shelter in his home out of cinderblocks and wood purchased locally. In addition to water, he stocked his shelter with emergency food and water kits for himself, his wife and his son. The food kits were manufactured by Surviv-All Inc. of New York City. Each kit included a gallon container of a protein mix called Multi-Purpose Food (MPF) that was created by General Mills. Enough nutrients and calories were provided in three scoops of MPF for one person per day. Although the mix could be eaten by itself, consumers were encouraged to combine it with juices or peanut butter, suggesting that MPF's taste left much to be desired. The kit was also stocked with fourteen water cans, one for each day of the two weeks that Americans might have to take refuge from radioactive fallout. After two weeks, emerging from fallout shelters was thought to be safe, and according to the Kansas Historical Society, "occupants were to emerge and forage the outside world for food." Shortly thereafter, the federal Department of Civil Defense undertook efforts in conjunction with state and local officials to locate and stock public fallout shelters. The Parman family never sought protection from fallout, but they did ride out the 1966 Topeka tornado in their basement shelter. In 2006, Dr. Parman donated one of his unused food kits to the Kansas Museum of History.[109]

President Kennedy assumed office appearing to view civil defense more urgently than President Eisenhower. In a May 25, 1961 "Special Message to Congress on Urgent National Needs," President Kennedy articulated his desire to strengthen the nation's civil defense and enhance the federal government's role in providing it:

> One major element of the national security program which this Nation has never squarely faced up to is civil defense. In the past decade we have considered a variety of programs, but we have never adopted a consistent policy....
>
> This administration has been looking very hard at exactly what civil defense can and cannot do. It cannot be obtained cheaply. It cannot give an assurance of blast protection that will be proof against surprise attack or guarantee against obsolescence or destruction. And it cannot deter a nuclear attack.

We will deter an enemy from making a nuclear attack only if our retaliatory power is so strong and so invulnerable that he knows he would be destroyed by our response....

But this deterrent concept assumes rational calculations by rational men. And the history of this planet is sufficient to remind us of the possibilities of an irrational attack, a miscalculation, or an accidental war which cannot be either foreseen or deterred. The nature of modern warfare heightens these possibilities. It is on this basis that civil defense can readily be justified—as insurance for the civilian population in the event of such a miscalculation. It is insurance which we could never forgive ourselves for foregoing in the event of catastrophe. [110]

To fund his new civil defense initiative, Kennedy followed this message by sending a July supplemental appropriations request of $207.6 million to Congress, which practically doubled the civil defense requests made during the Eisenhower presidency. Congress fully funded the request. The newly established Office of Civil Defense utilized the funds and began a nationwide survey to identify existing buildings to be used as fallout shelters and to stock them with supplies. [111]

Kansans in Reno County had a large fallout shelter under the courthouse in the county seat, Hutchinson, in which they could seek refuge. Built in the 1960s to hold more than 1,400 people in case of a nuclear attack, the facility was part of a huge 130-acre space, and the area where emergency supplies were stored was 650 feet underground, delivered by elevator. Another Reno County fallout shelter that could accommodate more than five times as many people was located underneath a grain elevator in the northeast part of the county. That facility could house 8,720 people during an attack. [112]

Fallout shelters were intended to protect citizens from radioactive nuclear fallout, which is what remains in the air after a nuclear explosion. "This dust is made radioactive by the nuclear explosion, and is blown miles downwind until falling back to earth. It then releases radioactivity until it decays." [113] If the Soviet Union had attacked the United States with nuclear bombs, even Americans who avoided injury or death from an explosion would have needed protection from drifting radioactive fallout until it decayed and no longer posed a threat. Shelters were intended to provide that protection.

To qualify as a public shelter—which would be marked with what became the familiar fallout shelter sign, three yellow triangles surrounded by a black circle—a space had to accommodate a minimum of fifty people, "include one cubic foot of storage space per person, and have a

The Far-Mar-Co. Inc. Elevator located in northeast Reno County. The county's largest fallout shelter, it could accommodate 8,720 people. May 1968. *Courtesy of Civil Defense Museum.*

radiation protection factor of at least 100." The Defense Supply Agency within the Department of Defense provided supplies to local governments, which assumed responsibility for stocking the shelters in their area. The Department of Defense created the federal fallout shelter sign in December 1961, and one was placed on each shelter that met the federal government's criteria.[114]

The October 18, 1961 edition of the *Salina Journal* carried a notice on page 2 that both Schilling AFB personnel and Salina civilians were encouraged to attend "a briefing on nuclear attack survival procedures" the next day at the base. The 1:30 p.m. instructional session in the base theater would be led by Schilling's disaster control officer Paul Gardella.[115] The same edition of the Salina newspaper included a page 1 Associated Press story about former president Dwight Eisenhower's unwillingness to be in a fallout shelter without his family. In that situation, Eisenhower said he would "just walk out" of the shelter that did not include his family members, even if they had experienced radiation exposure. "I wouldn't want to be left in that kind of a world," Eisenhower said. In response to whether he believed that national CD efforts were sufficient, he said that he had never known the correct answer to that question.[116]

A companion story on the same page of the newspaper referenced Willard F. Libby, winner of the Nobel Prize, and his answer to a question the previous day at a Los Angeles news conference about how to survive a nuclear bomb's fallout. Libby explained that rain carries fallout, but since little rain falls in the desert, it would be largely safe from fallout. Even though shelters would only "protect humans against local fallout but not against the long-range effects of radiation," since millions of humans would nevertheless be saved by seeking refuge in fallout shelters, they should be built.[117]

As continued evidence of national and local concern over the possibility of nuclear attack, one week later the newspaper carried an Associated Press story declaring that the ICBM sites like those near Topeka, Salina and Wichita would likely be targeted by the Soviet Union during a nuclear war. As a result, nearby locations would also be in danger from the effects of radioactive nuclear fallout. In fact, the story mentioned a 1960 study conducted by meteorologists revealing the likelihood of fallout adversely affecting the populations of locations near missile sites. According to the study, Kansas City stood a 50 percent chance of being affected by an attack on Salina's Schilling Air Force Base, and it also stood a 50 percent chance of being affected by an attack on Topeka's Forbes Air Force Base.[118]

Federal fallout shelter sign. *Courtesy of www.wikimedia.org.*

Even the U.S. military attempted to provide fallout protection for its personnel. In late October 1961, Deputy Secretary of Defense Roswell Gilpatric instructed the secretaries of the various branches to undertake actions that both protected service members and conveyed the seriousness with which the military took civil defense. Though money had not been allocated in the Defense Department budget for fallout shelters on military bases, some installations had begun designating existing space as fallout shelters. However, only the military members at the highest decision-making levels at locations such as the underground

Strategic Air Command headquarters at Omaha, Nebraska, and the personnel who operated the belowground ICBM launch sites had access to large shelters equipped to withstand the highest levels of radiation.[119]

Though Schilling Air Force Base had no fallout shelter construction projects, base information officer Lieutenant Tom Agee told the *Salina Journal* that it had for many years conducted briefings and even simulated nuclear attacks for the benefit of both base personnel and family members. Additionally, each house built in the Capehart housing addition, which was scheduled to open by the end of November 1961, included a basement, which would allow fallout shelters to be built under those homes more easily. Agee also said that the Schilling-area missile sites were built to withstand a nuclear attack, so they were fallout shelters.[120]

Evacuation was an option for Salina in case of a Soviet attack in late 1961. Assistant civil defense director Paul Bryant explained that the city's evacuation routes could be used to relocate Salina's citizens, including children and hospital patients, if an attack was believed to be imminent. Success depended on early evacuation, because he conceded that once an attack began, evacuation would not be possible. Bryant was confident that Schilling AFB would be targeted. "An enemy would try to hit it," he said. "The missile sites now under construction make this true of other parts of Kansas, too. Topeka and Wichita, for example, must be considered prime targets." He explained that, given enough time prior to an emergency, evacuation would work. Though he said that Salina's evacuation routes led to various locations where fleeing citizens could find housing and food, he did not specify what housing was available or where.[121]

In light of Cold War tensions heightened by the Berlin Crisis war scare of 1961, Nobel Prize–winning professor Willard F. Libby authored a fifteen-part series of articles for the *Salina Journal* titled "You Can Survive Atomic Attack." The November 3, 1961 edition announced the series of articles to begin the following Monday under the headline "This Advice May Save Your Life." Libby is described in the article as "America's best-known authority on fallout and radiation." The same article advertised Libby's lengthier book on the subject of surviving nuclear attack, which was available for fifty cents.[122]

Libby's second installment in the series listed several fallacies, each followed by facts that he provided to correct erroneous beliefs about surviving a nuclear war. The first fallacy dealt with the benefits of civil defense. "Fallacy: Defense is hopeless. Shelters cannot really help. Fact: Ninety to 95 percent of us survive, with proper protection." The next fallacy Libby addressed dealt with fallout. "Fallacy: Fallout 'poisoning' after a war would kill all life, everywhere. FACT: This is pure fiction. Deaths from local, close-in fallout could be very high if people didn't have fallout shelter protection. But the worldwide radiation levels, after a war, would have delayed effects just about comparable to those from the normal radiation levels in some parts of the world at present." Libby also addressed the notion that anyone within two or three miles of a nuclear bomb explosion would die. He conceded that although death was certain for anyone underneath a falling nuclear bomb, "fallout shelters could protect from blast many persons at marginal distances from the center" of the explosion. He also answered concerns that civilization would cease after cities were destroyed and agricultural land would be ruined by fallout. "FACT: Great areas would not be touched, including many cities and towns. We could rebuild destroyed areas, if people had not been sickened or weakened by radiation. That CAN be avoided. Intense fallout would not cover all our land, perhaps not more than 10 to 50 percent at most." Libby answered concerns about a nuclear bomb's radiation reaching several miles. "FACT: About two miles from a 10-megaton bomb. If you were that close, and unprotected, the blast and heat would kill you first, very likely." He also tried to allay concerns about future births. "FALLACY: All children in the future would be stillborn or genetic freaks, due to postwar fallout. FACT: Postwar fallout would produce some considerable rate of increase over the present rate of abnormal births, but most births would continue to be normal."[123]

The nuclear attack survival article in the November 8, 1961 edition explained how to build an inexpensive fallout shelter. Libby discussed his own thirty-dollar shelter, which he described as "a hole in a backyard hill, bags of dirt, and some railroad ties." The roof was twenty-eight inches thick and made of the railroad ties and dirt. He pointed out "that lethal X-rays from intensive fallout are stopped by two feet of concrete, or anything with equal density or mass." In an emergency, he suggested that seeking refuge under a table with concrete blocks or even layers of books placed on top of and stacked beside a sturdy table placed in the corner of a house's basement could save lives. Although an air filter would be ideal, only an insignificant amount of radioactive dust might enter. A radiation meter, however, was necessary. At a cost of twenty-five dollars, it would detect dangerous levels of fallout. Libby recommended that if dangerous radioactive dust became a problem, it should be removed with a broom. "Fallout eventually becomes ordinary dirt. But you must avoid or get rid of it while it is radioactive." A person who has sought safety in a shelter should remain inside of it for at least forty-eight hours after a nuclear explosion, though a two-week stay would ensure that radioactive fallout had declined to safe levels of exposure. For the person who would be enclosed in a small space for the first forty-eight hours, Libby recommended taking "sleeping pills to help wait out the most critical period of fallout danger."[124]

The same edition of the Salina newspaper carried an AP story on the same page about Henry Tutt, an enterprising Topeka man who was building a fallout shelter as rental property. Tutt appealed to the Topeka city commissioner for permission to build a shelter forty-five feet by forty-five feet with eight-inch walls and ceiling made of concrete reinforced with steel. Most of the shelter would be underground, although an air intake and chimney would be above. The city commission "granted Tutt a waiver of zoning regulation" to build his shelter, which he said he would offer as either a rental or lease basis.[125]

The next installment of the nuclear attack survival series by Libby explained the value of making a home fallout shelter as comfortable as possible to make a two-week stay more tolerable. According to Libby, a nuclear explosion's fallout radiation would not be lethal after the first two days, though it could cause illness or, with too much exposure, could eventually diminish a lifespan. He also declared that exposure could create a genetic effect for future generations. Libby claimed that his simple home shelter increased his chances of survival one hundred times. "But a $5,000 shelter could give 10,000-fold protection." Trying to outrun post-explosion fallout in a vehicle would be unwise, however. Instead of trying to flee, he recommended keeping a car's gas tank full, its windows closed and inside a garage to avoid exposure. If the car could not avoid exposure, the driver should remove the fallout atop the vehicle with a water hose before operating it. "And you might well keep some emergency supplies in it," Libby wrote, "including a shovel to dig foxholes if a renewed attack caught you out in open areas with a new cloud of fallout approaching." The same edition of the Salina Journal included a picture of a fallout shelter's interior with this caption: "An interior view of an underground shelter, elaborately equipped, that probably could be duplicated now for $8000. Shelters such as this can increase your chances 10,000 fold."[126]

The seventh article in Libby's series argued that, if a nuclear attack was imminent, children should leave school for either a home shelter or a public shelter, because few schools were equipped with fallout shelters. Children would be safer, and their parents' minds would be at ease. He also encouraged men who lived close enough to leave their jobs for the safety of home shelters, but those in metropolitan areas who would face massive traffic congestion in that situation should find a public shelter or seek shelter at work. Because advance warning of an attack seemed likely, Libby encouraged everyone to learn the civil defense siren patterns: "A steady siren tone lasting three to five minutes means an attack is believed imminent, and you should be ready for the blast and heat—early direct radiation effects. Three minutes of warbling sound, or short series of blasts of the siren, means attack is due any moment, and you should take cover."[127]

The twelfth installment encouraged parents to allow their children to become familiar with the family's fallout shelter. He even recommended that children be allowed to simulate living inside to prepare for the time when they would have to or, if only public shelters were an option, to let their children know their location. In addition to the necessities of life, shelters should be stocked with favorite children's games and toys to occupy their time and fight boredom during confinement. Libby also recommended that parents provide help for their children to sleep: "Sedatives can not only calm anxieties, but induce sleep to pass the critical hours." He ended the article with this realistic assessment: "Nuclear war would mean abolition of most comforts, and disruption of all normal routines, for children and adults alike. Preparations can reduce the shock and permit smoother adjustment to the shelter life which no one wants ever to see imposed upon us."[128]

Kansas State University assistant professor of engineering Raymond Hall began preparing to survive a nuclear attack in 1959 by planning for a fallout shelter to be installed on his property. Work began on October 1, 1961, and two months later, a discarded Union Pacific Railroad water tank had been turned into a family fallout shelter. The metal structure was buried in Hall's backyard and became a shelter thirty feet long and nine feet tall with a stairway, ventilated air with an exhaust to ensure fresh air circulated through the shelter and fifty gallons of water stored in a tank. The floor remained dirt to make garbage elimination easier in case the family was forced to remain in the shelter for an extended period. Like others of the era, the Hall family planned to use the shelter to store food and other items, house a deep freezer and provide an area for their children to play. Materials for the $1,150 shelter cost less than $200, and the rest was spent on labor and a crane with a large steel ball that was needed to remove dents the shelter sustained in transit to its backyard destination. When Hall was asked why he installed the shelter, he replied, "I think every head of a family has a moral obligation to protect his children. We have been warned that an attack may come, so we must be ready." Hall even invited the public to his home at 2121 Browning because he was willing to answer questions about the project.[129]

The U.S. Department of Defense published twenty-five million copies of a forty-eight-page booklet in late December 1961 for distribution at post offices and through both state and local CD groups in early January explaining how Americans could survive a nuclear attack. The book's foreword included a grim admission that in such an attack, millions of Americans would die; however, millions of others could survive. The Defense Department declared that, because of the nation's nuclear deterrent, a nuclear attack was not likely. "However, should a nuclear attack ever occur, certain preparations could mean the difference between life and death for you." The booklet gave instructions for how to prepare to survive an attack that included a five-megaton nuclear bomb—equal to the explosive power of five million tons of TNT. The booklet's goal was to inform citizens how to survive a nuclear explosion's radioactive fallout. "No hope is held out for those who happen to be within the range of the blast, heat and initial radiation of the fusion bomb," the booklet stated; within ten miles of a nuclear explosion "would be scenes of havoc, devastation and death." The goal was for survivors beyond the lethal blast zone to seek shelter from fallout and remain there for up to two weeks until leaving would be safe.[130]

The OCD created a handbook for citizens in January 1962 with instructions for building eight different kinds of home fallout shelters to be placed in basements or backyards to accommodate people who either lacked public shelter access or simply preferred shelter at home. The smallest shelter would accommodate three people and cost less than $75 to build, and the largest would accommodate ten people and cost approximately $550 to build. The design of each shelter was intended to be built as inexpensively as possible, which meant that most of the shelters required the homeowner to perform the construction. The eight different shelters were the "Basement Sand-Filled Lumber Lean-To Shelter," the "Basement Corrugated Asbestos-Cement Lean-To Shelter," the "Basement Concrete Block Shelter," the "Outside Semimounded Plywood Box Shelter," the "Belowground Corrugated Steel Culvert Shelter," the "Outside Semimounded Steel Igloo Shelter," the "Aboveground Earth-Covered Lumber A-Frame Shelter" and the "Belowground New Construction Clay Masonry Shelter." The last shelter was designed to be added to a new house under construction.[131]

The water drums provided by the federal government for local community shelters held seventeen and a half gallons of water. Each drum was intended to provide five people one quart of water a day for up to two weeks. Drums were made of either fiberboard or, later, steel, and each included two "plastic liners inside and stood about 22 inches tall and was about 16 inches in diameter." One liner held water, and the other liner was an extra to be used if needed. When filled with water, the polyethylene liners were either sealed with heat or tied. In normal conditions, the metal drums and polyethylene liners were expected to have a storage life of more than ten years.[132]

The Office of Civil Defense issued food guidelines in June 1964 for federally stocked fallout shelters. Though 1,500 calories consumed per day was determined to be sufficient to sustain daily activity for an individual, the government believed "that healthy persons can subsist for periods up to the maximum anticipated confinement of 2 weeks under sedentary conditions on a survival ration of 700 calories per day." The government considered seven requirements in determining appropriate fallout shelter foods:

> *The food* [must] *be palatable or at least acceptable to the majority of the shelter occupants; have sufficient storage stability to permit a shelf life of 5 to 10 years; be obtainable at low cost; be widely available or easily produced; have high bulk density to conserve storage space; require little or no preparation; and produce a minimum trash volume.*

Left: Civil Defense water drums in the basement of the Far-Mar-Co. Inc. Elevator, May 1968. *Courtesy of Civil Defense Museum.*

Opposite: J.W. Pedersen, civil defense director, Reno County, and Homer J. McConnell, representative of the Office of Civil Defense (Industrial Participation), Washington, D.C., examine emergency rations and supplies stored by the City of Hutchinson at the Underground Vaults and Storage Inc. facility, 650 feet below ground, May 1968. *Courtesy of Civil Defense Museum.*

Above, left: East entrance of Reno County Courthouse. Fallout shelter was located in the basement and could accommodate 1,415 people, May 1968. *Courtesy of Civil Defense Museum.*

Above, right: Reno County Courthouse Civil Defense Office secretary Joan Beery and civil defense director J.W. Pederson discuss distribution of public fallout shelters in Hutchinson. May 1968. *Courtesy of Civil Defense Museum.*

Left: Civil defense sign on wall in corridor leading to the Reno County Courthouse Civil Defense Office, May 1968. *Courtesy of Civil Defense Museum.*

In light of these criteria, the Armed Services Forces Food and Container Institute chose four items with which to stock shelters: the "Survival Biscuit," the "Survival Cracker," the "Carbohydrate Supplement" and the "Bulgur Wafer." They were packaged separately in sealed cans with an estimated shelf life of between five and fifteen years.[133]

In addition to stocking shelters with food and water, the federal government also stocked each community shelter with a medical kit. Initially developed

Civil defense supplies in the Reno County Courthouse Civil Defense shelter. This was a dual-use facility also used as a lunchroom, May 1968. *Courtesy of Civil Defense Museum.*

in the 1962 fiscal year and slightly altered after the 1966 fiscal year, they were provided for physical ailments, including emergencies, as well as for "controlling emotional stress." The supplies fell into three categories: "Medication," "Dressings" and "Other." The medication included aspirin, Eugenol, eye and nose drops, isopropyl alcohol, kaolin and pectin mixture, penicillin, petrolatum, phenobarbital, surgical soap, sodium bicarbonate, sodium chloride and sulfadiazine. The dressings included bandages, gauze, muslin, purified cotton and surgical pads. Other items included cotton-tipped applicators, tongue depressors, forceps, safety pins, scissors, thermometers and an instruction manual. The general storage life in normal conditions for the items was estimated at a minimum of five years and a maximum of at least ten years, with all of the dressings and most of the Other items listed as having an indefinite storage life.[134]

A crowd of five hundred to six hundred people attended the March 31, 1962 variety show and dance fundraiser for Salina civil defense called *Operation Survival*. The event raised $600 to transport and store supplies for

Above: City of Hutchinson–Reno County Civil Defense Emergency Operating Center located in the basement of the Reno County Courthouse. Equipment shown includes a teletype unit, typewriter, speaker units, radio units, converters, telephones and linear amplifiers. Secretary Joan Beery operates the teletype unit, May 1968. *Courtesy of Civil Defense Museum.*

Opposite, top: Boeing Company–Wichita Division security guard standing in front of entrance designated by shelter signs over doors that opened to a passageway leading to a civil defense shelter. This Wichita underground shelter was stocked to accommodate six hundred people, May 1968. *Courtesy of Civil Defense Museum.*

Opposite, bottm: Fire extinguisher, emergency telephones, medical supplies and more in a dual-use tunnel and fallout shelter stocked to accommodate five hundred people in the Boeing Company–Wichita Division plant, May 1968. *Courtesy of Civil Defense Museum.*

Salina's public fallout shelters. Saline County civil defense director Marie Webb said that a survey had identified 120 buildings in Salina that could serve as public fallout shelters, and the buildings' owners were being contacted for permission to use them in case of attack. Shelters would be modified to increase protection from radiation, after which each would be supplied with enough food, water and "sanitary facilities" for two weeks, along with equipment to monitor radiation. Although the federal government

Above: Intersection in dual-use tunnels and fallout shelters in the Boeing Company–Wichita Division plant. These tunnel-shelters could accommodate twelve thousand people, May 1968. *Courtesy of Civil Defense Museum.*

Opposite, top: Security guard Harold Thompson examining emergency supplies in a wall case in a dual-use tunnel and fallout shelter in the Boeing Company–Wichita Division plant, May 1968. *Courtesy of Civil Defense Museum.*

Opposite, bottom: Security guard Harold Thompson examines radiological instruments stored in a wall cabinet in dual-use tunnel and fallout shelter in the Boeing Company–Wichita Division plant, May 1968. *Courtesy of Civil Defense Museum.*

would provide the shelter supplies, Salina would have to pay to store and transport them until the shelters were ready to receive them. According to the April 2, 1962 edition of the *Salina Journal*, "The Salina Jaycees, Kiwanis, Rotary, Cosmopolitan and wives' clubs from Schilling AFB" helped with *Operation Survival*. In addition, the "Schilling AFB Officers' Wives club donated $100." Locals provided the entertainment, including "the Salina High 'Symphonettes'; Salina High Choral group, 'The Mellowtones'; the Marymount 'Azure Ayres'; Schilling 'Drifters' and the Kansas Wesleyan University Comic Ballet group."[135]

In light of the October 1962 Cuban Missile Crisis, Salina's CD contingent readied for a Soviet nuclear attack. The Sunday, October 28 edition of Salina's newspaper reported that, according to Marie Webb, only 4,500

Opposite, top: Security guard Harold Thompson tests emergency Civil Defense telephone in dual-use tunnel and fallout shelter in the Boeing Company–Wichita Division plant, May 1968. *Courtesy of Civil Defense Museum.*

Opposite, bottom: Fallout shelter sign marking entrance into hallway off east distribution area. This hallway led into the cafeteria shelter at the Boeing Company-Wichita division plant, May 1968. *Courtesy of Civil Defense Museum.*

Above: Dual-use snack bar and fallout shelter in the Boeing Company–Wichita Division plant cafeteria. The shelter could accommodate 1,500 people, May 1968. *Courtesy of Civil Defense Museum.*

Salinans, or 10 percent of the city's population, could be accommodated in the city's fallout shelters. Although twenty-four city buildings had been approved by the federal government as possible public fallout shelters, only nine were actually ready for use, and none of them had been provisioned with food or medicine. Webb did not know when the supplies would arrive in the shelters.[136] (By February 1966, however, eighty-four designated public fallout shelters that could accommodate 34,000 people had passed federal muster. Only about fifty of them had been provisioned with survival supplies, though.)[137] Salina and Saline County communications via ham radio were also being readied amid the October 1962 nuclear war scare. Robert A.

Office of Civil Defense sanitary supplies and medical kits stored in Boeing Company–Wichita Division plant, May 1968. These supplies were intended to sustain twelve thousand people for fourteen days. *Courtesy of Civil Defense Museum.*

Lang, "radio officer for the Central Kansas area," told the newspaper that three stations were available to both transmit and receive signals—one for a fifteen-county area around Salina, one for the city and Saline County and one that would allow direct communication with the state capital in Topeka. The ham radio operators who were members of the Central Kansas Radio Club were scheduled to meet the following Friday to discuss their communications role should the situation create an emergency.[138]

Neola H. Stillwell built an extensive fallout shelter on his Scottsville farm in Mitchell County. In the wake of the Cuban Crisis, the *Salina Journal* reported in late November 1962 that Stillwell's motivation to build his shelter included his belief that north-central Kansas would be targeted in a nuclear war because of the Atlas E and F missile sites near Schilling AFB and Forbes AFB. Stillwell equipped his $5,000-plus shelter with a ham radio; a "fallout meter"; hundreds of pounds of dehydrated, powdered and canned food; kitchen equipment that included a deep freezer full of pies, ice cream and beef; a coffee maker and cookstove and plenty of plates in a cupboard;

and a bathroom with medicine and shaving necessities. He provided the shelter with sources of gasoline and electricity. The facility also included a ventilation system to filter air, two oxygen tanks in case a blast eliminated the filtered air and two escape hatches to supplement the traditional method of exiting. As a ham radio operator, Stillwell answered roll call each afternoon at 12:30, along with about forty other radio operators in Kansas as well as Oklahoma and Nebraska. The newspaper reported that they maintained a watch for suspicious activity in the areas where they lived. The article ended on a somber note as Stillwell seemed to convey a belief in the inevitability of nuclear conflict, but he admitted that neither he nor anybody else knew when the Soviet Union's nuclear-tipped ICBMs would start landing.[139]

Salina hosted a day-long civil defense area briefing on Monday, December 16, 1963, in the Memorial Hall fallout shelter. Approximately 140 officials and administrators from seventeen north-central Kansas counties attended the event, which included an address by E. Norman Harold with a Kansas State University civil defense training program. Harold emphasized "the need for continuity of government and leadership" during a nuclear war. "For example, if you feel the county seat would be eliminated in case of a nuclear attack, then you must provide for another place of government to be used," Harold said. He also said that even though as many as 250 million Americans could die in a nuclear attack, fallout shelters could save 50 million. The Kansas State University training group held fifteen civil defense seminars around Kansas. The Salina seminar was attended by the Kansas civil defense director Warren Paramore of Topeka, the Saline County Commissioners chairman Keith Hughes, Salina mayor Gaylord Spangler and Saline County civil defense director Marie Webb.[140]

Salina's readiness preparations included a civil defense voice warning system. On June 28, 1964, Saline County civil defense director Marie Webb announced that the system would be tested on July 9 at 10:00 a.m. The Altec Lansic Corporation manufactured the system equipment that Salina used, and company district representative Tom Rooney from Kansas City was scheduled to be present for the test. The county civil defense office purchased the Altec equipment through McClelland Sound Company of Wichita. Webb said that the loudspeakers would be used first to announce the test, immediately after which the warning sound, described as a "siren-like tone," would also be tested. Webb said that a three-minute siren tone would signal the alert, after which the "warbling or 'up-and-down' tone" would sound for three minutes. "This is the signal that would mean 'take cover' if it were an alert," Webb said. The test's completion would be announced after a statement by a civil defense official. Webb said that the test would be broadcast over Salina's twelve loudspeakers, located "at city hall, the North 5th street water tower, St. John's Military school, Salina Concrete Products Co., Sunset school, South Park school, the Sunset water tower, South Junior High School, Heusner school, Salina high school, Marymount college and Gleniffer Hill school." Webb said that due to city population growth, six more speakers were needed.[141]

The March 30, 1965 edition of the Kansas State University student newspaper, the *Kansas State Collegian*, announced that twenty fallout shelters had been designated in as many campus buildings and could accommodate nineteen thousand people. The story referenced civil defense training program supervisor Norman Harold, who told the newspaper that the Department of Defense provided "medical, food and sanitation supplies" and radiological equipment to stock the campus shelters.

The story relayed that a thirty-two-hour shelter management training program was provided by the university that included overnight stays in fallout shelters located throughout Kansas. Course instructor Lee Boumaker conveyed to the student newspaper that one thousand people had taken the course, and although it was not yet an accredited program, it might become one. Each campus fallout shelter and its capacity were listed:

> *Farrell library, 235; Willard hall, 1,085; Kedzie hall, 1,515; Agricultural Engineering building, 415; Presbyterian Student Center, 125; Justin hall, 2,570; Thompson hall, 510; Student Health Center, 590; Physical Science building, 4,659; the Union, 4,205; PI BETA Phi, 320; Farm-House, 275; Kappa Sigma, 175; Sigma Alpha Epsilon, 205; Delta Delta Delta, 140; Tau Kappa Epsilon, 125; Women's Residence Hall, 660; Men's Residence Hall, 735; Boyd Hall, 415; and Putnam Hall, 415.*[142]

The Kansas State University power plant's whistle was first used as a civil defense siren on April 5, 1965, when it was sounded during a monthly test in Manhattan. The student newspaper reported that, according to Manhattan city manager D.C. Wesche, the city would continue alerts the first Monday of the month April through October, at 10:00 a.m. Similar tests would follow in 1966, beginning with one test in January; monthly tests would resume in April. Each test would include a continual one-minute siren sound followed by a silent minute, after which, according to the story, "a rising and falling wail or a series of short blasts will be sounded to denote the take cover signal." The siren sounds to warn Manhattan residents of an actual nuclear attack

Hope Library, formerly Farrell Library, one of the designated fallout shelters on the campus of Kansas State University in Manhattan. *Courtesy of www.wikimedia.org.*

would be slightly different—a continual wail would blow from the siren for five minutes as the alert, and after a silent minute, a continual three-minute wail would indicate that the residents needed to take shelter immediately.[143]

Because civil defense was such an important part of the Kansas consciousness, Saline County 4-H members attended a 4-H civil defense meeting in July 1966. The members were addressed by county CD director Marie Webb. She stressed the importance of all citizens contributing to civil defense and its importance during natural disasters and war. She even showed the educational movie *About Fallout*. The 4-H meeting was held in the county fallout shelter, and Webb gave the students a tour of the expansive facility.[144]

Jerry Boettcher was a nuclear engineer in the early 1960s. Shortly after the Cuban Missile Crisis, he went to work for Kansas State University. His mission was to travel the state and educate people about building fallout shelters. The Kansas State program was funded by a U.S. Department of Defense grant. "I was in a different town every night," Boettcher said in a 2016 interview. "It was a lot of work, all that driving. I was living in Manhattan, Kansas, so if you go somewhere like Colby, Kansas, that's 270 miles." Boettcher's

Right and below: Kedzie Hall, one of the designated fallout shelters on the Kansas State University campus in Manhattan. *Courtesy of www.wikimedia.org.*

The Union, one of the designated fallout shelters on the Kansas State University campus in Manhattan. *Courtesy of www.wikimedia.org.*

students were often municipal employees or people affiliated with hospitals and universities. He wanted to teach them to teach others. "The subject was interesting to me, and my challenge was to try to make it interesting to them so they could feel comfortable instructing others," he said. In addition to teaching about the ideal materials and locations for shelters, Boettcher also carried samples of radioactive materials to communicate the dangers of radiation exposure. His most memorable class was also his largest, and it met in Dodge City on November 22, 1963. "I remember that because I was unloading the car at my motel when I turned on the TV and heard Walter Cronkite saying the president (Kennedy) had been shot," Boettcher said. Before cellphones and email, communication options were limited, and he had to decide if class would be canceled in light of that day's events in Dallas. "Because many people drove from other communities, I would have had to have stayed just to say, 'We're not having class.' So we went ahead and had class that morning." After a career in investment analysis, in 2007 Boettcher became a member of the Kansas Board of Regents.[145]

Jerry Boettcher taught civil defense classes across the state for Kansas State University in the 1960s. He is seen here standing by the Triga Mark II Nuclear Reactor facility on the KSU campus in Manhattan. *Courtesy of Kansas State University Global Campus Alumni Link Magazine, Fall/Winter 2016 issue.*

When President Kennedy was assassinated in November 1963, space for 110 million shelters had been identified around the nation, of which 70 million were available for use and 14 million were stocked with supplies. However, the first year of Lyndon Johnson's presidency, Congress appropriated only $105.2 million of the OCD's requested $358 million. By 1968, the final year of Johnson's presidency, the amount requested fell to $77.3 million, of which Congress appropriated only $60.5 million. According to Blanchard, the lack of support for civil defense—caused by the acceptance of the philosophy of mutual assured destruction, the fear that civil defense preparations would actually trigger nuclear war and the prohibitive costs of the Vietnam War—from President Johnson and Secretary McNamara influenced Congress to withhold support as well.[146]

As the late 1960s became the 1970s, the two superpowers entered an era of détente. Although the Cold War persisted, the United States and Soviet Union managed to peacefully coexist. In spite of this, the danger remained until the presidency of Jimmy Carter. Manhattan columnist Mike Matson was born in that city just two months after the Soviet Union launched Sputnik in 1957. As he ruminated in a June 30, 2019 column for the *Mercury*, two years after his birth, his father, a Kansas State graduate, made sure that the family house he had built in Rooks County included "a sub-basement below the normal basement, complete with four bunks and canned peaches." As a twenty-something Wichita DJ in 1979, one of Matson's radio station duties was to record government messages for the Emergency Broadcast System—the ones that began, "This is not a test." "The rest was official language," Matson wrote with twenty-first-century detachment, "that basically amounted to: 'If you're still alive and listening to this radio station, hang in there. Despite the unfortunate circumstances related to the end of the world, you remain an essential cog in your country's doctrine of Mutual Assured Destruction. Oh, and don't eat the peaches if the cans are rusty.'"[147]

The forty-five-year conflict called the Cold War ended quietly for the United States in the early 1990s without a nuclear cataclysm. In fact, it ended without a nuclear weapon being fired at an enemy. The anticlimactic ending stood in stark contrast to decades of danger, fear and, at times, panic that gripped Kansans, particularly during the crisis years of the early 1960s as the Cold War entered its most dangerous period, the apex of which was the Cuban Missile Crisis of October 1962, when the world stood on the precipice and looked into an abyss. The Cold War mantra of civil defense preparedness became ingrained in Kansas's collective consciousness as the state's communities joined national civilian preparedness efforts to survive a nuclear attack during the Cold War's most dangerous years.

DWIGHT EISENHOWER

COLD WAR PRESIDENT

Dwight David Eisenhower was born on October 14, 1890, in Denison, Texas, but the next year, the Eisenhower family moved to Abilene, Kansas. Eisenhower and his five brothers—Arthur, Edgar, Roy, Earl and Milton—were raised in the family home situated at 201 South East Fourth Street. Eisenhower graduated from Abilene High School in 1909, and after earning a satisfactory score on the service academy exam, he entered West Point in 1911 and graduated in 1915. The following year, he married Mamie Doud of Denver. Eisenhower remained in the United States during World War I training troops in San Antonio, Georgia, Maryland and Gettysburg, Pennsylvania. He did, however, receive the Distinguished Service Medal for his wartime service.[148]

Having risen to the rank of major, Eisenhower was sent to study at the Command and General Staff School at Leavenworth, Kansas, in 1925. He finished his course of study top of his class, after which he was transferred to the War Department in Washington, D.C., where he worked for General John J. Pershing, who sent Eisenhower to the Army War College and then to Paris. In 1929, he was sent back to Washington as aid for Army Chief of Staff General Douglas MacArthur, with whom he spent the next ten years. Eisenhower became a lieutenant colonel in 1936, a full colonel (temporary) in March 1941, then brigadier general (temporary) the following September. Then, following the Japanese attack of Pearl Harbor on December 7, 1941, Eisenhower was summoned from Fort Sam Houston, Texas, to the War Department in Washington, where he began working directly under Army

Abilene boyhood home of Dwight D. Eisenhower. *Courtesy of www.wikimedia.org.*

Chief of Staff General George C. Marshall developing global war plans for the United States. In March 1942, General Marshall recommended that Eisenhower be promoted to major general (temporary).[149]

Because of Eisenhower's outstanding abilities, General Marshall named him commander of the European theater of operations in June 1942. Eisenhower's command post was London, where he oversaw all American forces in the theater. Having begun overseeing American and British troops during Allied operations in the Mediterranean, in February 1943, Eisenhower was promoted to full general, and his four-star rank was then the army's highest. Then, in December 1943, President Franklin Roosevelt named Eisenhower the supreme commander of Operation Overlord, the Allied invasion of German-occupied Normandy that began on June 6, 1944. Eisenhower was promoted to general of the army, which was a five-star rank. With Overlord's success, by March 1945, Eisenhower's Allied Expeditionary Force had fought through German resistance and was within approximately two hundred miles of that nation's capital, Berlin; the Soviet army, however, was only thirty-five miles away. Distance, the casualties that

Dwight D. Eisenhower's high school graduation portrait, 1909. *Courtesy of Dwight D. Eisenhower Presidential Library, Museum & Childhood Home.*

would be sustained and the decision reached by the leaders of the United States, Great Britain and the Soviet Union at the Yalta Conference the previous February to divide conquered postwar Germany into occupation zones—with Berlin in the eastern zone to be controlled by the Soviet Union—helped Eisenhower decide not to attempt to beat the Soviet troops to Berlin. Surrounded by the Allies and defeated, Germany surrendered in May 1945. According to Eisenhower biographer Stephen E. Ambrose, "Overlord was the greatest amphibious assault in history, with the largest air and sea armadas ever assembled." In the words of General Marshall, Eisenhower had achieved "the greatest victory in the history of warfare," having "commanded with outstanding success the most powerful military force that has ever been assembled." According to Ambrose, Eisenhower "was the most successful general of the greatest war ever fought."[150]

Following the war, Eisenhower held five different professional positions prior to retirement. He served as head of America's German Occupation Zone, army chief of staff, Columbia University president, supreme commander of NATO forces and president of the United States. As early as 1945, Eisenhower was sought by both Democrats and Republicans to be each party's presidential candidate, and even President Truman vowed to help him win the 1948 presidential election. In fact, in 1947, President Truman offered to be Eisenhower's vice-presidential running mate if he would allow the Democratic Party to nominate him as its presidential candidate. Eisenhower had come to view Soviet actions in Eastern Europe as repressive and proof of its intent to spread its Communist rule. He foresaw a conflict with the United States and even wanted to go beyond the Truman administration's Containment policy to roll back Communism and reclaim nations enslaved behind the Iron Curtain, yet he declined President Truman's unique offer. Then, in November 1951, President Truman again offered to help Eisenhower secure the Democratic presidential nomination, which he again declined for, among other reasons, his being a Republican. That political party came calling as well, and Eisenhower listened. By

As supreme commander of the Allied Expeditionary Force, General Dwight D. Eisenhower speaks with paratroopers of the 101st Airborne Division just before they board their planes to participate in the Normandy invasion, June 5, 1944. *Courtesy of www.wikimedia.org.*

February 1952, Eisenhower was convinced to run for the Republican Party's presidential nomination. With Richard Nixon as his running mate, Eisenhower promised on October 24, less than two weeks before the nation voted, that, shortly after his election, he would go to Korea as a first step to ending the war there. This nearly guaranteed his November 4, 1952 election victory over Democrat Adlai Stevenson. Three days before the election, the United States detonated its first hydrogen bomb, which was 150 times stronger than the atomic bombs dropped on Hiroshima and Nagasaki at the end of World War II. President Eisenhower assumed leadership of the United States as the Cold War became considerably more dangerous.[151]

President Eisenhower conceded the danger in his January 20, 1953 inaugural address. In a speech entirely about foreign policy, he said that his administration would seek peace, but it would do so in a world where "forces of good and evil are massed and armed and opposed as rarely before in history." The Korean War was being fought with conventional

Above: Dwight D. Eisenhower views homecoming parade in Abilene, Kansas June 6, 1952. *Courtesy of Dwight D. Eisenhower Presidential Library, Museum & Childhood Home*

Left: President Eisenhower and Vice President Nixon during the January 20, 1953 inaugural ceremonies. *Courtesy of Dwight D. Eisenhower Presidential Library, Museum & Childhood Home.*

weapons, but as destructive atomic weapons were giving way to even more destructive thermonuclear weapons, Eisenhower warned his hearers of the dangers that the United States and the world faced as the Cold War moved into its newest phase. The president ominously intoned that "science seems ready to confer upon us, as its final gift, the power to erase human life from this planet."[152]

On the heels of Joseph Stalin's March 5, 1953 death, Eisenhower hoped to announce his intention to live peacefully with the Soviet Union in his first post-inauguration address as president. Eisenhower delivered "The Chance for Peace" speech to the American Society of Newspaper Editors at Washington's Statler Hotel on April 16, 1953. He declared his concern over both the expense and the threat to world peace that a continued arms race meant, the ultimate threat being a nuclear war. He characterized the circumstances of living on such a permanent war footing as "humanity hanging from a cross of iron."[153]

President Eisenhower entered office in January 1953 determined to end the war in Korea. By the following June, the Chinese Communists, who had entered the fighting alongside Communist North Korea, communicated a desire to end the fighting and agreed to a cease-fire line near the prewar boundary separating North Korea and South Korea at the thirty-eighth parallel. By July 26, a truce had been signed, shortly after which President Eisenhower informed the nation through a television and radio address. Ambrose wrote that Eisenhower was intent on ending the conflict because he "realized that unlimited war in the nuclear age was unimaginable, and limited war unwinnable. This was the most basic of his strategic insights."[154]

President Eisenhower opened his October 8, 1953 press conference by announcing that the Soviets had, for the first time, tested a hydrogen bomb. He told the press that the Soviet Union now possessed "a stockpile of atomic weapons…and the capability of atomic attack on us, and such capability will increase with the passage of time." Eisenhower went on to assure the American public, however, that the nation's atomic arsenal was significant and growing.[155]

The afternoon of December 8, 1953, President Eisenhower delivered his "Atoms for Peace" speech to the United Nations General Assembly in New York City. He informed the UN and the world that the United States' atomic bombs were twenty-five times stronger than the atomic bombs dropped on Hiroshima and Nagasaki in 1945 and that American hydrogen bombs equaled the power of millions of tons of TNT. Since 1945, the United States had test exploded forty-two atomic and nuclear bombs, and the American "stockpile of atomic weapons, which, of course, increases daily, exceeds by many times the explosive equivalent of the total of all bombs and all shells that came from every plane and every gun in every theater of war in all of the years of World War II." He conceded, however, that the Soviets were racing to catch up, and continuing such an arms race "would be to confirm the hopeless finality of a belief that two atomic colossi are doomed malevolently to eye each other indefinitely across a trembling world."[156] There had to be a better way. He suggested, therefore, that both the United States and the Soviet Union agree to remove atomic weapons from war arsenals and devote use of the atom to peaceful purposes—the United States, Great Britain and the Soviet Union should donate atomic materials from their stockpiles to an International Atomic Energy Agency that would be set up within the United Nations to, among other uses, provide electricity to energy-deficit parts of the world. The Soviets ignored the speech, but the International Atomic Energy Agency was finally created in 1957.

Because the Soviets rejected the "Atoms for Peace" plan, Eisenhower made the hydrogen bomb the focus of his military policy as he implemented his "New Look" defense plan. Fearing that by 1954 the Soviet Union would have acquired a hydrogen bomb, in 1950 President Truman anticipated raising defense spending beyond $50 billion annually. Eager to cut defense spending, President Eisenhower wanted to spend less money on defense by increasing the nation's nuclear arsenal while cutting back on traditional forces. This meant expanding the air force role and relying on American nuclear superiority over the Soviets. Referring to the nation's nuclear capability in a January 1954 speech, Secretary of State Dulles said that the president and his National Security Council had decided that the United States would respond to national security threats with "a great capacity to retaliate instantly by means and places of our own choosing." President Eisenhower was deeply concerned about a surprise Pearl Harbor–style Soviet nuclear attack, and he made clear that he would act immediately within this philosophy of "massive retaliation."[157]

With French forces fighting against Communists in Vietnam, President Eisenhower was intent on helping the French stave off Communist domination in Southeast Asia. Remembering the finger pointing and the cries of "Who lost China?" when that nation fell to Communists in 1949 during the Truman presidency, he wanted to avoid similar blame. However, he also wanted to avoid introducing American ground troops in what was then called Indochina because he feared heavy casualties that would be sustained in the jungle fighting. By early 1954, the U.S. government was paying approximately 75 percent of the French bill for fighting there, and President Eisenhower authorized two hundred air force personnel to accompany the ten bombers he was sending to the French in Southeast Asia. Eager to formalize the expansion of the policy of containment there, at an April 7 news conference, President Eisenhower announced the "Domino Theory." In response to a question about Indochina, the president said that the nations there were similar to a row of dominoes, and if the first were knocked over and fell to Communism, the rest would quickly fall. He believed that if Indochina fell, other regional countries would fall; Japan, Formosa and the Philippines would be next, and this would threaten both Australia and New Zealand. After the French defeat at Dien Bien Phu in May 1954, the subsequent partition of Vietnam with Communists in the north and the French in the south, followed by the French withdrawal, Eisenhower worked to create the Southeast Asia Treaty Organization (SEATO), and he announced the nation's support for new South Vietnamese leader Ngo Dinh Diem.[158]

The surprise Pearl Harbor attack on December 7, 1941, made a lasting impression on Dwight Eisenhower. He knew that in the atomic age, a surprise attack could mean destruction on an unheard-of scale. Desperately needing intelligence about Soviet nuclear capabilities, President Eisenhower formed the Surprise Attack Panel, headed by MIT president James R. Killian, with Polaroid camera inventor Edwin H. Land as a member. Land had told Eisenhower that cameras were sophisticated enough to take clear photos from extremely high elevations. Kelly Johnson with the Lockheed Company suggested building a reconnaissance airplane that could fly at seventy thousand feet. He called it the U-2 ("utility aircraft number two"). CIA director Allen Dulles, Killian and Land liked the idea, and they paid President Eisenhower a visit on November 24, 1954, during which they asked permission to spend $35 million to build thirty U-2s. Eisenhower granted permission to proceed, but he predicted that eventually the Soviet Union would down one of them, "and we're going to have a storm."[159]

Five times in 1954—twice over Dien Bien Phu in Vietnam in April and May, once in June because the French relayed that China would soon enter the fighting there, again in September when China began shelling the Quemoy and Matsu Islands near Formosa and finally in November when China announced that captured American pilots would serve prison sentences—the National Security Council, Joint Chiefs of Staff and Department of State recommended dropping atomic bombs on China. Each time, Eisenhower declined to do so. Though Eisenhower stated in a March 1955 press conference that he would consider using "tactical small atomic weapons" in war in that part of the world and compared those atomic bombs to bullets, in late spring 1954, he told South Korean president Syngman Rhee, who also encouraged using atomic weapons in the Far East, that doing so would be awful. "Atomic war will destroy civilization," Eisenhower said. "War today is unthinkable with the weapons which we have at our command. If the Kremlin and Washington ever lock up in a war, the results are too horrible to contemplate. I can't even imagine them."[160]

Eisenhower's fear of a surprise nuclear attack reflected the 1950s tension brought on by knowledge that the Soviets possessed long-range bombers that could deliver unimaginably destructive hydrogen bombs and were building submarine-launched and intercontinental ballistic missiles that could do the same. Unable to match Soviet conventional military superiority, Eisenhower wanted to press the American nuclear advantage, yet building more bombs provoked the Soviets to follow suit. To ease the arms race and exorbitant spending, at the Geneva Summit with the Soviet leadership in July 1955, the American president proposed that the United States and Soviet Union allow each other to overfly its territory for reconnaissance missions to verify that neither country was clandestinely increasing its nuclear striking capability and mobilizing for war against the other. However, First Secretary of the Communist Party Nikita Khrushchev rejected Eisenhower's "Open Skies" proposal as an American attempt to spy on the Soviet Union, and the idea was never realized.[161]

Though it reflected the American obsession with automobiles in the mid-1950s, the interstate highway system—called President Eisenhower's "principal domestic legacy" by biographer Evan Thomas—also reflected American Cold War concerns with survival. President Eisenhower pitched the idea to Congress as a way to evacuate large, heavily populated cities in the event of a Soviet nuclear attack.[162]

Following the 1954 American hydrogen bomb tests in the Pacific, the Atomic Energy Commission told the president that bombs could be made small enough to fit inside missiles that could be delivered long distances, after which Eisenhower directed the development of missiles be intensified. He invested $500 million in missile development in 1955 and asked for $1.2 billion for missile development in 1956. More than doubling the amount invested in missiles was necessitated by pursuing both intermediate range ballistic missiles (IRBMs) that could travel 1,500 miles and intercontinental ballistic missiles that could travel much farther. While the air force pursued the Atlas and Titan ICBMs, the navy pursued the Thor, and the army

President Eisenhower receives a report from Lewis L. Strauss, chairman of the Atomic Energy Commission, on the hydrogen bomb tests in the Pacific, March 30, 1954. *Courtesy of www.wikimedia.org.*

pursued the Jupiter IRBMs. In spite of increased missile spending, in February 1956 Missouri senator Stuart Symington alleged that the United States mightily trailed the Soviet Union in missile development, and the first charges were made that President Eisenhower allowed a "missile gap" favoring the Soviets to develop. Eisenhower rebutted the charge during a February 8, 1956 press conference: "Can you picture a war that would be waged with atomic missiles…?" He then answered the question, echoing what he had said during his first inaugural address and to President Rhee: "It would just be complete, indiscriminate devastation, not [war] in any recognizable sense, because war is a contest, and you finally get to a point [with missiles] where you are talking merely about race suicide, and nothing else."[163]

At the beginning of 1956, Eisenhower was considering running for a second presidential term, and international tensions helped him decide. According to historian David A. Nichols, after meeting with Secretary of

President Eisenhower's official photo portrait, July 1956. *Courtesy of www. wikimedia.org.*

State Dulles on January 10, Eisenhower wrote in his diary that day that they had been unable to find proof that the world was moving in the direction of "peace and disarmament" and "that it would appear that the world is on the verge of an abyss." Then, less than two weeks later, shocking information reached the president that further solidified this viewpoint and reinforced his decision to run for reelection. The Net Evaluation Subcommittee of the National Security Council delivered a report to President Eisenhower that he had requested listing the damage that the United States and the Soviet Union would sustain in a nuclear war between the two nations. In a hypothetical attack, Eisenhower was told that the U.S. economy would be ruined for up to a year; the federal government's leaders would likely all be killed, leaving the states to somehow create one anew; and most joltingly, 65 percent of the nation's people would be dead or dying, with the latter unable to get needed emergency medical care. Being told that the United States would visit three times the devastation on the Soviet Union brought

President Eisenhower no comfort, because, he said, Americans "would literally be…digging ourselves out of ashes, starting again." Accepting the Republican nomination for president at the Republican National Convention the following August, Eisenhower echoed these concerns when he told the assembled delegates in San Francisco, likely with the Net Evaluation Subcommittee report in mind, that the existence of nuclear weapons meant that "war has become, not just tragic, but preposterous. With such weapons, there can be no victory for anyone."[164]

The year that Eisenhower ran for a second term was fraught with international danger that included a nuclear war scare. The 1956 Suez Crisis, which peaked as Americans went to the polls in November, resulted when the Eisenhower administration withdrew financial support for Egyptian leader Gamal Abdel Nasser to build the Aswan Dam after Nasser embraced China's Communist government and bought arms from Soviet satellite Czechoslovakia. When Nasser nationalized the Suez Canal and began operating it to fund building the dam, the British and French, fearful that the Egyptians could not be trusted to allow Western European nations continued access to the canal, conspired with Israel to provoke a confrontation that would allow the British and French to resume control of the canal. Israeli troops entered the Sinai Peninsula and advanced west toward the canal in late October. After Egyptian troops engaged the Israelis, the British and French issued an October 30 ultimatum: either stop fighting and accept British-French occupation and control of the canal, or they would secure their objective militarily. British bombing began the following day. Behind the Iron Curtain, Polish and Hungarian protests against Soviet control broke out as Eisenhower campaigned in early November. Then, on November 5, British and French troops landed on Egyptian soil, and the Soviet Union responded by threatening Great Britain, France and Israel with a nuclear attack if the Anglo-French forces did not immediately cease their invasion of the new Soviet ally. The Soviet leader even wrote to Eisenhower suggesting that the two countries' armies should jointly move troops into Egypt and end the fighting. Instead, Eisenhower readied the American military to repel a Soviet invasion there, even if it meant using nuclear weapons. "If those fellows start something, I'll have to hit 'em—with *everything* in the bucket if necessary," Eisenhower told his top advisors. The following day was Election Day, and Eisenhower again defeated Democrat Adlai Stevenson, his 1952 opponent. That same day, Eisenhower spoke to British prime minister Anthony Eden, who had declared that the British agreed to a ceasefire, ending the Suez Crisis. A nuclear war was averted, but the Soviets had brutally suppressed Budapest protests and killed forty thousand Hungarians in the process, discouraging protests in all its puppet states.[165]

The Soviet Union launched the world's first ICBM in August 1957. Two months later, the Soviets shocked the American public by launching Sputnik, the first ever artificial satellite, into orbit on October 4. Americans feared falling behind the Communist nation educationally and technologically. Nikita Khrushchev told the *New York Times* that the Soviets would soon churn out ICBMs "like sausages." Eisenhower faced aggressive questions from the press and criticism from Democrats wanting to know how he was going spur the nation to catch up to the Soviets, and pressure was placed on Eisenhower to spend increasingly large sums on a national fallout shelter program and expanded nuclear weapons production. Eisenhower resisted the pressure. By June 1958, he received some help resisting the pressure from the CIA. The agency admitted that it had dramatically overestimated Soviet bomber and ICBM production in August 1956 when it predicted that by the middle of 1958 the Soviets would have 470 bombers and 100 ICBMs. The CIA estimated that in June 1958, the Soviets had only 135 bombers and not a single operational ICBM.[166]

According to Ambrose, Eisenhower inherited about 1,500 nuclear weapons in 1953. By 1959, that number had risen to about 6,000, and Ambrose characterized the "American ability to hit the Russians" as "already awesome" then. Yet the Joint Chiefs of Staff requested $50 billion for the 1960 fiscal year; the Department of Defense lowered that number to $43.8 billion, and President Eisenhower wanted it still lower at $40 billion. Given the size of the American nuclear striking power and the ability of the nation to retaliate against a nuclear attack, Eisenhower asked, "How many times do we have to destroy Russia?" U-2 reconnaissance missions over the Soviet Union in 1956 and '57 showing the absence of increased nuclear striking power reinforced Eisenhower's determination to hold down defense spending, but he could not tell Congress or the American public about the bonanza of spy-plane intelligence. The Soviets knew of the U-2 overflights and also chose not to inform the public, but they did discreetly lodge protests as they told American officials that their radars tracked each CIA plane crossing Soviet territory.[167]

On November 10, 1958, Soviet leader Nikita Khrushchev issued a six-month deadline for the Allies to leave West Berlin, or the Soviet Union would sign a peace treaty with East Germany eliminating Allied access rights in the western portion of the capital city. President Eisenhower disagreed;

he argued that the 1945 Yalta agreements that had established Allied access rights in the western half of the city were still in effect and would remain so. Khrushchev charged that once a Soviet–East Germany treaty was signed, the East German government would force the Allies out of Berlin, risking war with that Communist nation and, ultimately, the Soviet Union. Confident that Khrushchev would back down, Eisenhower remained firm and denied that a Berlin Crisis existed to calm public fear. Before the six months had elapsed, in March 1959, President Eisenhower repeatedly explained to the Joint Chiefs of Staff, Republican leaders and Democratic leaders that this was just another Soviet attempt to upset Americans and keep the nation agitated, and he told his audiences that "the Communist objective is to make us spend ourselves into bankruptcy." Instead of singling out the Berlin Crisis as unique, everyone should understand it within the larger, long-term conflict between the two nations. "This is a continuous crisis," Eisenhower said, "that the United States has to live with certainly as long as we are going to be here." He explained that the best American strategy meant patiently and firmly standing against the Soviets as the Communist system was undermined from within and ultimately destroyed, which he said could take forty years. The six-month deadline came and went, and Khrushchev proved Eisenhower right by doing nothing.[168]

Cuban Fidel Castro led a group of rebels and overthrew that country's leader, Fulgencio Batista, in January 1959. Although the United States recognized the new Cuban government, Castro legalized the Communist Party, executed Batista supporters and began denouncing the United States. President Eisenhower encouraged the CIA to begin thinking of ways to remove Castro from power. In March 1960, Eisenhower approved a CIA "program" for Cuba that started with creating a Cuban government-in-exile and included covert operations on the island nation and establishing "a paramilitary force outside of Cuba for future guerrilla action." Training for that guerrilla action was expanded and given a $13 million budget, but executing the action would fall to Eisenhower's successor. Shortly before leaving office, however, President Eisenhower severed relations with Cuba's government in January 1961.[169]

The pressure on President Eisenhower continued and intensified in his final year in office. In 1960, he was repeatedly asked by the press why the country failed to do more to catch up with the Soviets and if he feared a Soviet nuclear attack. He publicly declared that no missile gap existed, just as no bomber gap had existed three or four years earlier. According to Evan Thomas, in "1960, the United States had a dozen ICBMs and about 1,500

Left: President Eisenhower's official photo portrait, May 1959. *Courtesy of www.wikimedia.org.*

Below: President Eisenhower and Soviet leader Nikita Khrushchev at the Soviet embassy in Washington, D.C., September 1959. *Courtesy of www.wikimedia.org.*

long-range bombers. The Soviet Union had two ICBMs and about 120 long-range bombers." To journalist Charles Shutt, Eisenhower answered charges that he was endangering the nation by placing fiscal philosophy ahead of security and failing to develop needed weapons: "I don't believe we should pay one cent for defense more than we have to," Eisenhower said. "Our defense is not only strong, it is awesome, and it is respected elsewhere." President Eisenhower knew that the United States maintained a considerable lead in weapons development over the Soviets, but he was precluded from telling the world how he knew. CIA pilots had flown the top-secret U-2 on reconnaissance missions over the Soviet Union several times, and the photographs taken during those flights proved that the Soviets were not mass-producing ICBMs. To move toward world peace, Eisenhower wanted to sign a test-ban treaty with Khrushchev and achieve a level of disarmament before his presidency ended.[170]

Eisenhower's hopes for such agreements with the Soviet Union were dashed by an ill-fated U-2 flight over the Soviet Union in May 1960. The president had authorized an April 9 overflight that was picked up by Soviet radar—just as U-2 flights had been since the first one in 1956—

Kelly Johnson of the CIA (*left*) and pilot Francis Gary Powers in front of a U-2. *Courtesy of www.wikimedia.org.*

and Soviet military personnel attempted to shoot down the spy plane with surface-to-air missiles (SAMs) without success. Even though Eisenhower and Khrushchev had agreed to meet at a Paris summit meeting in mid-May to discuss disarmament and other matters, because the CIA wanted photographs of a possible ICBM launch site, the president authorized one last pre-summit U-2 flight over the Soviet Union. On May 1, the Soviets shot down the U-2 flown by American pilot Francis Gary Powers. President Eisenhower was informed and led to believe that the airplane and the photographic film were destroyed and the pilot was dead, none of which was true. Khrushchev publicly announced that the U-2 had been shot down and that the Soviet government had the airplane's salvaged parts and the pilot in its custody. The incident forced the president to reveal to Congress the existence of the U-2 and to admit to the American people and the world that the nation had in fact spied on the Soviet Union. President Eisenhower justified the overflights at a subsequent press conference by declaring that national security required intelligence about Soviet nuclear capabilities, but the Communist nation's secrecy made spying "a distasteful but vital necessity." Of course, the Soviet Union also had satellites flying over the United States at the same time. Khrushchev launched an angry denunciation of Eisenhower and the Americans during the first summit session at Paris, and then he left, taking with him Eisenhower's hopes for a disarmament deal during his presidency.[171]

The evening of January 17, 1961, three days before John F. Kennedy was sworn in as the new president, Eisenhower gave his farewell address to the nation, which was broadcast on television and radio. He spoke of the Cold War. "We face a hostile ideology, global in scope, atheistic in character, ruthless in purpose, and insidious in method," he said. The hostility faced would be of "indefinite duration." He reminded his audience that the nation's historically small military had grown tremendously along with the influence of the private defense industry that supplied that military with weapons: "We have been compelled to create a permanent armaments industry of vast proportions." He warned the nation to avoid spending itself into bankruptcy. "This conjunction of an immense military establishment and a large arms industry is new in the American experience," Eisenhower said. "In the councils of government, we must guard against the acquisition of unwarranted influence, whether sought or unsought, by the military-industrial complex. The potential for the disastrous rise of misplaced power exists and will persist." He said that this new, powerful entity should not be enabled to "endanger our liberties

Left: Soviets look at U-2 exhibit, May 1960. *Courtesy of Dwight D. Eisenhower Presidential Library, Museum & Childhood Home.*

Below: Wreckage from the U-2 flown by Francis Gary Powers that was shot down over the Soviet Union in May 1960 on display at the Central Museum of the Armed Forces in Moscow. *Courtesy of www. wikimedia.org.*

The Eisenhowers' Gettysburg, Pennsylvania farmhouse. *Courtesy of Dwight D. Eisenhower Presidential Library, Museum & Childhood Home.*

or democratic processes. We should take nothing for granted." He spoke of the failure to reach disarmament: "I confess that I lay down my official responsibilities in this field with a definite sense of disappointment. As one who has witnessed the horror and the lingering sadness of war—as one who knows that another war could utterly destroy this civilization which has been so slowly and painfully built over thousands of years—I wish I could say tonight that a lasting peace is in sight." Though he could not, he could say that "war has been avoided."[172]

Evan Thomas wrote that President Eisenhower "was the first person in history to have the means to wreck civilization." Yet he spent his presidency in the years 1953–61 trying to avoid war to preserve that civilization. "Having done as much as any man to win World War II, Ike devoted the rest of his public service to keeping America and the world out of World War III." Thomas believed that the nation was "blessed to be led by a man who understood the nature of war better than anyone else, and who had the patience and wisdom, as well as the cunning and guile, to keep the peace."[173]

Above: President Lyndon Johnson and Dwight D. Eisenhower aboard Air Force One, October 5, 1965. *Courtesy of www. wikimedia.org.*

Left: White House portrait painted by James Anthony Wills, 1967. *Courtesy of www. wikimedia.org.*

Stephen Ambrose characterized Dwight D. Eisenhower as a complex individual who "exuded simplicity. He deliberately projected an image of the folksy farm boy from Kansas. But in fact he was capable of detached, informed, and exhaustive examination of problems and personalities, based on wide and sophisticated knowledge and deep study." Having suffered multiple heart attacks, by March 1969, Eisenhower was under medical care at Walter Reed Hospital and he was exhausted. He had decided that he would be buried across the street from his childhood home in Abilene, near his presidential library and museum. On March 28, with his wife, son and grandson by his side, shortly before his tired heart stopped beating, he looked at his son and said, "I want to go." In Ambrose's words, Eisenhower "was ready to go home, back to Abilene, back to the heart of America, from whence he came."[174]

6

KANSAS MILITARY INSTALLATIONS

The Cold War saw the birth of at least one Kansas Air Force Base. Some of the state's other military installations began during World War II, while the oldest trace their roots to the nineteenth century. All were important to the state and the nation during the Cold War as military personnel were prepared to defend the nation against attack or travel overseas in service to the country.

FORBES AIR FORCE BASE

Only two weeks after the Japanese attack on Pearl Harbor in December 1941, Congress granted permission to create the Topeka Army Air Field (TAAF). With construction finished, the U.S. Army Air Corps assumed control of the facility the following August, and the first troops arrived shortly thereafter. The 333rd Bombardment Group made TAAF home the next month, and by 1945, it was just one of three locations nationally from which B-29 crews left for the Pacific in new Superfortresses to invade Japan at the end of World War II. Following the war, TAAF was inactivated October 31, 1947.[175]

Because of the Cold War, TAAF became a Strategic Air Command base on July 1, 1948, after which it was renamed Forbes Air Force Base in honor of Topeka pilot Major Daniel H. Forbes, who was killed in June 1948 while flying a Northrop bomber in California. The 311th Air Division and the 55th

LOOKING NORTH on "F" Street, main dormitory area at Forbes AFB. A grain elevator in Pauline is at upper left.

Forbes Air Force Base dormitories. *Courtesy of www.wikimedia.org.*

Strategic Reconnaissance Wing were based at Forbes AFB until October 14, 1949 when the base was once more inactivated.[176]

The base reopened as a SAC base during the Korean War. The 21st Air Division stood up at Forbes on February 16, 1951, and that month and the next that division's 90th Bombardment Wing also arrived. Between June 1951 and August 1953, the base trained new bombardment wings and B-29 crews as they prepared for combat. On June 16, 1952, the 90th Bombardment Wing became the 90th Strategic Reconnaissance Wing. In October 1952, the 55th Strategic Reconnaissance Wing relocated from Ramey AFB in Puerto Rico to Forbes AFB and continued specializing in photography and reconnaissance. Then, in June 1960, the 90th Strategic Reconnaissance Wing was replaced by the 40th Bomb Wing, which arrived from Schilling Air Force Base at Salina, until 1964. Tactical Air Command assumed control of the base in 1965.[177]

Forbes AFB became the hub for nine Atlas E missile sites that were built beginning in June 1959, and the 548th Strategic Missile Squadron stood up at Forbes on July 1, 1960. With construction complete at all nine sites and an Atlas E missile stored at each, the sites were activated in October 1961. Because the Atlas program was soon phased out and the missile sites decommissioned by the Department of Defense, the 548th Strategic Missile Squadron at Forbes was deactivated on March 25, 1965. The Department of Defense closed the base in 1973. The site was transferred to the City of Topeka in 1976 for commercial flight use and for use by the Kansas Army National Guard. In 2012, Forbes Field's name was changed to Topeka Regional Airport & Business Center.[178]

Topeka felt the economic and demographic benefits of Forbes AFB. When the base closed in 1973, more than $32 million in annual income was earned by five thousand base personnel and civilian employees, which contributed greatly to the local economy. Half of the five thousand base employees and their six thousand dependents lived in Topeka, Carbondale, Lyndon and other nearby communities. In spite of the economic loss, Ron Keefover of Topeka remembered a sense of relief when the base closed, because the threat of being targeted in a nuclear attack diminished. "There was just some remote tension about that being a SAC base and then being a potential target for international enemies," Keefover told the *Topeka Capital Journal* in 2013. "I think I remember breathing a little easier when the SAC part was decommissioned." The shuttering of Forbes AFB did not seem to affect the area population, though. Between 1970 and 1980, Topeka's population dropped by only 0.51 percent, and Shawnee County's population dropped by only 0.03 percent.[179]

FORT LEAVENWORTH

Fort Leavenworth is among the oldest military installations in the country. Established in 1827 by Colonel Henry Leavenworth and his men of the 3rd Infantry Regiment of St. Louis's Jefferson Barracks, the fort was used during the war with Mexico in 1846, after which it supplied various military camps, one supply depot and multiple forts. The site was an office for Governor Andrew Reeder in 1854, and its soldiers were engaged in the era's "Bleeding Kansas" episode. Camp Lincoln was established there and trained Kansas volunteers during the Civil War. Afterward, Leavenworth reverted to its role in supplying Western forces. The U.S. Army Command and General Staff College was begun at Fort Leavenworth during the late nineteenth century. Its notable graduates include General George S. Patton Jr. as well as fellow World War II and Cold War military leaders General Omar Bradley and President Dwight D. Eisenhower.[180]

FORT RILEY

Fort Riley's roots can be traced to at least 1853, when it was a stopping point for settlers traveling west on the Santa Fe, California and Oregon Trails. Because of its location in the middle of the country, it was originally called "Camp Center," though its name was changed to Fort Riley in honor of Mexican War hero Major General Bennett C. Riley.[181] Lieutenant Colonel George Armstrong Custer assumed command of the 7th Cavalry at Fort Riley in 1866, and in 1892, the School of Cavalry and Light Artillery began operating there. Then, in 1907, the Mounted Service School began there, though after World War I the name was changed to the Cavalry School. Notable trainees who passed through Fort Riley's schools include General George S. Patton Jr.[182]

Fort Riley housed German prisoners of war during World War II, when the fort added thirty-two thousand acres to its property. Among the 125,000 soldiers who trained at Fort Riley during that war were actor Mickey Rooney

Custer House at Fort Riley. Courtesy of Fort Wiki, www.fortwiki.com.

Patton Hall at Fort Riley. *Courtesy of www.wikimedia.org.*

and heavyweight boxing champion Joe Louis, both of whom went on to serve in Special Services, which entertained troops.[183] Fort Riley saw the arrival in 1955 of the 1st Infantry Division from Germany, necessitating the addition of fifty thousand acres to its property. The 1st Infantry Division sent troops to fight in Southeast Asia between 1965 and 1970. The fort also sent troops to Germany in the 1970s and 1980s to defend our West German and Western European allies from a possible Soviet invasion.[184]

McConnell Air Force Base

The United States Air Force created Wichita Air Force Base after it assumed control of Wichita Municipal Airport in 1951 to train combat crews on the B-47 Stratojet for service during the Korean War. Colonel Henry R. Spicer's 3520th Combat Crew Training Wing trained crews there for the Boeing B-47 Stratojet bomber. One piece of base construction christened in August 1952 was the chapel, which remains in use. The air force spent $22 million on base construction between 1954 and 1956, which, in addition to other projects, included nearly five hundred housing units, paved roads and hangars. At a May 15, 1965 ceremony, the base's name was formally changed to McConnell Air Force Base to honor Fred and Tom McConnell, brothers who flew in the Army Air Corps during World War II. The 4347th Combat Crew Training Wing, part of Strategic Air Command, replaced the 3520th on July 1, 1958.[185]

The 42nd Strategic Aerospace Division stood up at McConnell AFB on July 15, 1959. Then, thirteen months later, the USAF allocated $1 million to build access roads and supply utilities for the Titan II intercontinental ballistic missile launch sites that would be attached to McConnell AFB. On November 29, 1961, the 381st Strategic Missile Wing was activated there, and the 388th Tactical Fighter Wing was also activated at McConnell on October 1, 1962. The 42nd Strategic Aerospace Division was inactivated on July 1, 1963. Tragedy struck the base on January 16, 1965, when a KC-135 Stratotanker that had arrived from Clinton-Sherman Air Force Base in Oklahoma crashed in a Wichita neighborhood shortly after takeoff, killing thirty people, including the entire seven-person crew. Another tragedy occurred on March 5, 1974, when another KC-135 Stratotanker seven-person crew died in a crash caused by mechanical malfunction during take-off. Two years later, on August 23, 1976, one of the Kansas Air National Guard's F-105 Thunderchiefs crashed, and both crew members were killed. Almost two years to the day later, August 24, 1978, two missile maintenance crew members at a Titan II ICBM site were killed due to a fuel oxidizer leak. In response to the Department of Defense decision to phase out the Titan II, the first McConnell-area missile was taken off alert to begin the deactivation process on July 2, 1984, and the 381st Strategic Missile Wing and related units were inactivated on August 8, 1986. Then, on April 26, 1991, an F-3 tornado struck the base and irreparably damaged more than one hundred houses, McConnell's hospital and several other structures. Although sixteen injuries were reported, no deaths were sustained.[186]

SCHILLING AIR FORCE BASE

Because of the need created by World War II, construction began on Smoky Hill Army Air Field at Salina in April 1942. The base was primarily used for B-17 bombers and later as a training base for the B-29 Superfortress. Though inactivated in April 1950, the base was reactivated one year later

Boeing-Wichita
B-29 Assembly Line,
1944. *Courtesy of*
www.wikimedia.org.

in response to the Korean War. The 40th and 310th Bombardment Wings were assigned there in 1952. The base was renamed to honor Colonel David Carl Schilling, a native Kansan who was an accomplished pilot and an innovator who, according to a base history published by Schilling AFB, "first proved the global strikeforce concept a reality by in-flight refueling of two F-84 jet fighter aircraft" in September 1950 when the "two F-84s flew non-stop from Manston Air Base near London, England to Mitchell Field, New York." The 40th and 310th Bombardment Wings were transferred to Topeka's Forbes AFB in 1960.[187]

The 550th Strategic Missile Squadron and its twelve Atlas F intercontinental ballistic missile sites became operational in October 1962 just in time for the Cuban Missile Crisis. The 550th SMS was the nation's first such squadron to operate ICBMs that were stored entirely underground in reinforced vertical silos. The previous March, the 310th Bombardment Wing was renamed the 310th Strategic Aerospace Wing and, according to the base history written in the first half of the 1960s, with "its squadrons of [B-47] bombers, tankers and missiles and the numerous support and tenant organizations, Schilling continues to be one of the most important bases in the Free World's strongest peace force—The Strategic Air Command." The first time that the Stratotanker was based in Kansas was when the first KC-135 arrived at Schilling on March 7, 1964. The KC-135s allowed jet-to-jet aerial refueling for Schilling AFB's bombers.[188]

When the Atlas missile program was phased out, the need for Schilling AFB ended. Salinans learned on November 19, 1964, that the base would close by the end of June 1965, and fear spread that the loss of the economic engine that powered the local economy would decimate the city. According to a November 16, 2014 *Salina Journal* story, the base "employed 763 officers, 4,244 airmen and 357 civilians." With the base closing, those jobs—and the revenue that they generated and was spent locally—would leave. Rumors of base closure had begun swirling early in 1964, prompting Kansas representative Bob Dole to seek clarification from the USAF about its plans for Schilling AFB. The January 4, 1964 *Salina Journal* reported that Brigadier General Perry M. Hoisington II told Dole "that the Air Force has no plans to close or drastically curtail operations at Schilling Air Force Base." By November, however, Schilling was among ninety-five military sites that Secretary of Defense Robert McNamara had scheduled to close.[189]

Although Salinans feared that the closure would bring economic catastrophe, it did not. In his 1966 master's report surveying the economic impact on Salina of Schilling Air Force Base's closure, Kansas State University graduate student Donald W. Lorenzo found that Salina rebounded nicely. While he found that even though the presumed economic loss to Salina from the loss of Schilling AFB's thirteen thousand personnel and family members—about twenty-five percent of Salina's population—and their $20 million of payroll, much of those losses were, in a relatively short time, offset. Although home construction and real estate sales did diminish, other sectors of the local economy recovered. The federal government stepped in to help those military personnel who were making mortgage payments but were forced to transfer. About 2,700 houses in Salina were put up for sale between December 1964 and June 1965, and selling was difficult. To forestall defaults and foreclosures and to ease the financial burden on transferring personnel, the Federal Housing Authority and Veterans Administration assumed responsibility for defaulted properties, and they paid off the amounts owed, which stopped some loss of revenue.[190]

Sales declined 9 percent from the period including the base closure announcement in November 1964 through the actual closure in June 1965 compared to the same time frame a year earlier. Salina's newspaper lost three thousand subscribers during approximately the seven months following the announcement of Schilling AFB's closure, but subscriptions rebounded to within eight hundred of the number of subscribers just before the announcement. The Salina school system lost the $500,000 in annual aid paid by the government to schools located in communities with military personnel who were exempt from paying the taxes that were earmarked for those schools.[191]

Ironically, Salina's business community came to view the base closure as beneficial. By June 1966, Salinans had accepted that an air force base in their city was unlikely, and they worked together to make the city succeed without a military presence. In fact, many had come to believe that the city had become dependent on the USAF and had transitioned to recruiting private business and industry unrelated to the military. Soon after the base closure was announced in November 1964, members of Salina's business community met with Representative Dole, U.S. senator Frank Carlson, Salina's Mayor Carl Rundquist and chamber of commerce president Carl Engstrom to chart a path forward. Then, on December 15, several people, including Mayor Rundquist, Carl Ramsey of the Saline County Commissioners, Superintendent of Salina Public Schools W.W. Ostenberg, members of the Salina Chamber of Commerce, Salina's City Manager Norris Olson and *Salina Journal* editor Whitley Austin along with Representative Dole, Senator Carlson and Governor-elect William H. Avery met with Deputy Secretary of Defense Cyrus Vance, Secretary of the Air Force Eugene Zuckert and Don Bradford, director of economic adjustment, in Washington, D.C., to lobby for Salina. At this meeting, a group from the nation's capital was chosen to travel to Salina and provide guidance on methods by which the economic losses of base closure could be ameliorated. One of the meeting's results was that plans were put in motion to use the federal property being vacated by the USAF for local economic development.[192]

According to Lorenzo, transitioning to a civilian-based economy had, by June 1966, offset the economic losses associated with base closure by creating "a far more reliable (because of diversification) group of industries and other activities than Schilling Air Force Base proved to be." Additionally, several people who lived in surrounding areas who were reluctant to do business in Salina with the military base there had begun patronizing Salina businesses following the closure. In fact, by the summer of 1966, deposits in local banks had returned to pre-closure levels, and Lorenzo characterized Salina as "thriving" and "optimistic," with a "growing" economy, and he finished his graduate research with this complimentary opinion: "To have transformed spears into plowshares in such a relatively short time is a feat worthy of recognition. It is to be hoped that the other cities affected by the Same Department of Defense Order will be able to follow Salina's shining example."[193]

A slightly less rosy assessment was given by the *Salina Journal* in 2014. It pointed out that Salina's 1950 population was 26,176, its 1960 population had grown to 43,202 and a 1962 University of Kansas study forecast that

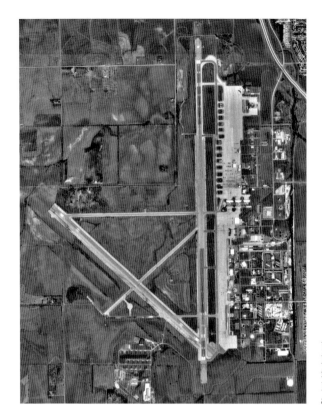

USGS photo of Salina Municipal Airport, formerly Schilling Air Force Base. *Courtesy of www.wikimedia.org.*

Salina's 1965 population could climb to 50,000; yet, by 1970, Salina's population had fallen to 37,714. In fact, the city's 1990 population still had not rebounded to reach its 1960 numbers. The population did, however, climb to those numbers and beyond by 2010. A vocational technical school moved to the base after closure, and it became and remains the Salina Area Technical College. After acquiring Schilling, the City of Salina turned the base into an industrial complex and utilized existing infrastructure to create what the Salina newspaper called "a municipal airport with runways and taxiways that larger cities would come to envy."[194]

Kansas has a unique history of military service, and this history includes five military installations that were key to maintaining the nation's security during the Cold War, three of which operated ICBMs as part of the nation's nuclear arsenal. As the home of U.S. Air Force and U.S. Army forces, these installations prepared to defend the nation at home and fight abroad. Forbes Air Force Base, Fort Leavenworth, Fort Riley, McConnell Air Force Base and Schilling Air Force Base bolstered the nation's defenses and ensured its safety during a crucial era.

THE DAY AFTER

The Day After aired on ABC the evening of Sunday, November 20, 1983, to an audience exceeding 100 million viewers. The made-for-TV movie depicted the impact of a nuclear war between the United States and the Soviet Union by showing the destruction of Kansas City and how the people in Lawrence, Kansas, and western Missouri coped with the aftermath. These areas of Kansas and Missouri were selected because of their central location, but the number of ICBM launch sites in both states made them likely Soviet targets in an actual nuclear attack, which added credibility to the story.[195]

Director Nicholas Meyer told an interviewer years after the movie aired that he didn't make the movie as entertainment; instead, he considered it a public service announcement. One writer argued that much of the movie's effectiveness as that public service announcement is because its cast comprised normal people instead of actors. Meyer intended to forego using any known stars, but he relented to ABC, who needed some known actors to sell the movie overseas. Jason Robards plays Dr. Oakes, who, shortly after the nuclear attack, makes his way back to the University of Kansas to tend to the living wounded. Hollywood up-and-comers JoBeth Williams, John Lithgow, Stephen Furst, Amy Madigan and Steve Guttenberg also appear. Broadway actor and future *Northern Exposure* star John Cullum also landed a role, and he was chosen to appear on ABC just prior to the movie's airing to warn viewers that they would see some "unusually disturbing" things in the next two hours.[196]

The movie's attack scene features Kansas City, and many city landmarks are shown, including the Kansas City Stockyards, Union Station, the Country Club Plaza, Liberty Memorial, the University of Kansas Medical Center and the Truman Sports Complex. The St. Joseph Hospital was being demolished at the time, and its actual rubble appears in one of the movie's scenes, and the fictionalized remnants of a destroyed Liberty Memorial appear as well.[197]

The post-attack scenes center on Lawrence, Kansas, and northwestern Missouri, where dying survivors cling to life amid the destruction and the resulting chaos that includes martial law following the elimination of most civil government. Mental health professionals around the country fielded thousands of hotline calls from viewers who had been upset by the movie. ABC News also aired a special broadcast as soon as the movie ended that included political pundits and scientists who discussed the possibility, causes and likely consequences of an actual nuclear war. Kansas City's ABC affiliate KMBC-TV also aired the program *Sunday, Nuclear Sunday*. In a poll taken following *The Day After* and these televised follow-ups, 44 percent of people in and around Kansas City said that they would likely live to see a nuclear war. Mirroring national anti–nuclear war sentiment, approximately 1,200 activists met for a vigil at Liberty Memorial, and other public anti-nuclear events were held around Kansas City. Nuclear war survival was the message of companies that installed shelters.[198]

Much of the movie's cast—including University of Kansas faculty and students—were locals, including more than sixty who landed speaking roles. The use of locals in Lawrence where much of the movie was shot was intentional to depict the horrors that nuclear war would visit on average Americans. By the movie's end, most of the characters depicted by Kansans had died or were barely alive. The movie's final hour depicts the nuclear attack on Kansas City and the aftermath of survivors, and ABC chose not to broadcast any commercials during that hour. The 100 million viewers represented about two-thirds of that night's television audience, and the broadcast still ranks as one of the most-viewed televised programs in history.[199]

Author Dawn Stover described the process of transforming Lawrence into the post–nuclear attack focus of the second half of the movie:

> *To turn Lawrence into a war zone, the film's producers closed sections of Massachusetts Street (downtown's pedestrian-friendly main street, lined with shops and trees) more than once, blew out the windows of storefront, gave buildings a charred makeover, and littered downtown with ash, debris,*

Left: Liberty Memorial in Kansas City. *Courtesy of www.wikimedia.org.*

Middle: Truman Sports Complex in Kansas City. *Courtesy of www. wikimedia.org.*

Bottom: Kansas City Stockyards. *Courtesy of www.wikimedia.org.*

and burned-out vehicles. A few blocks from downtown, the filmmakers built a tent city to house "refugees" under a bridge on the banks of the Kansas River, known locally as the Kaw. Each tent housed a family and some of the possessions they had presumably taken when they fled from devastated homes: a doll here, a radio there.

Retired University of Kansas theater professor Jack Wright cast the movie's extras, and his stepdaughter plays the role of twelve-year-old "Joleen." In a 2018 interview, Wright said that walking "from tent to tent" felt "like going through a neighborhood." He also described how Allen Fieldhouse, where the University of Kansas basketball teams play home games, was filled with cots to shoot scenes for the movie's dying fallout exposure victims. According to Wright, in addition to reminding the amateur actors who filled the extra roles not to look at the camera during filming, director Nicholas Meyer also told the Kansans that in the event of a real nuclear war, "nobody would leave this room alive. You're on your last legs."[200]

The movie attempts to convey the post-attack carnage as it shows Kansans dying of radiation poisoning, including losing their teeth and hair as they stagger amid burned fields littered with dead animals. While the credits roll at the movie's end, the message is that all of the carnage and ruin depicted in the movie was "in all likelihood, less severe than the destruction that would actually occur." Lithgow's character is a university professor who quotes Albert Einstein: "I know not with what weapons World War III will be fought, but World War IV will be fought with sticks and stones."[201]

When *The Day After* aired in 1983, Wichita's McConnell Air Force Base was still the hub for 18 Titan II missiles. These were the largest ICBMs that the United States deployed. Missouri's Whiteman Air Force Base, to the east of Kansas City, was the operational hub of 150 Minuteman II ICBMs, which is why the movie shows Lawrence residents watching Minuteman missile vapor trails in the skies above the South Park gazebo. The attack on Kansas City includes bright flashes as mushroom clouds ascend after explosions, which is when the government footage of actual missile tests supplement the Hollywood nuclear simulations, and viewers see a "rapid-fire series of 'skeletonized' people instantly killed in the midst of everyday activities."[202]

Commentator Sean O'Neal argues that the scene depicting the nuclear attack remains compelling, because it intersperses actual footage of government missile tests with scenes that include Kansans "watching ominous vapor trails appear over gazebos in the park, before being flash-frozen in the

Allen Fieldhouse on the campus of the University of Kansas in Lawrence. *Courtesy of www. wikimedia.org.*

blast." In a 2017 article about the movie, which aired when he was only five, O'Neal wrote why the movie so affected him after so many years as an adult: "Maybe it's the sentimentality brought on by new parenthood, but I haven't been able to shake the image of a mother holding her baby as they're transformed into glowing X-ray skeletons, evaporated in an instant."[203]

The Day After had a profound impact on United States president Ronald Reagan, who, after viewing the movie the month before it aired, recorded in his personal diary that watching the movie "left me greatly depressed.… My own reaction was one of our having to do all we can to have a deterrent & see there is never a nuclear war." In fact, after Reagan signed the 1987 Intermediate-Range Nuclear Forces Treaty (INF) with Soviet leader Mikhail Gorbachev, which eliminated an entire class of nuclear weapons, the president sent Meyer a message: "Don't think your movie didn't have any part of this, because it did."[204]

Following a relaxation of Cold War tensions in the post–Cuban Missile Crisis 1960s through the détente years of the 1970s, *The Day After* aired during a time of renewed Cold War fears in the early 1980s. In fact, two months earlier, the Soviet Union's missile-detection system falsely reported that American nuclear missiles had been launched toward the Communist nation. Fortunately, Soviet colonel Stanislav Yevgrafovich Petrov recognized the false alarm and did not initiate a retaliatory nuclear strike. Then, just two weeks before the movie aired, the United States and its NATO allies engaged in the nuclear-attack simulation Able Archer exercise that included military aircraft being "armed" with mock nuclear warheads. Able Archer was the culmination of the Autumn Forge NATO exercise, which included a military buildup in Europe. The Soviet government was unaware that these actions were merely drills and believed that NATO was preparing to launch a nuclear attack. As a result, the Soviet military in East Germany and Poland was, for the first time, placed on highest alert. Fortunately, the Soviet Union chose not to launch its own attack.[205]

The same month that *The Day After* aired—November 1983—NATO began supplying West Germany with American Pershing II missiles. All of Europe was within range of Soviet medium-range missiles, and the Pershing missiles were deployed as a counterbalance. The nuclear war depicted in *The Day After* is triggered by European conflict escalation, and the movie even includes a Soviet official talking of the "coordinated movement of the Pershing II launchers." The 1987 INF Treaty signed by President Reagan and General Secretary Gorbachev eliminated these missiles by prohibiting all conventional and nuclear missiles with ranges between 310 and 3,420 miles.[206]

Just two days before the movie aired on ABC, President Reagan wrote of a Situation Room briefing that he received about the American nuclear attack plan. Then, in his autobiography seven years later, he mentioned the movie in writing about the briefing:

> *Simply put, it was a scenario for a sequence of events that could lead to the end of civilization as we knew it. In several ways, the sequence of events described in the briefing paralleled those in the ABC movie. Yet there were still some people at the Pentagon who claimed a nuclear war was "winnable."*[207]

Two days after the movie aired, Secretary of State George Shultz appeared on an ABC program with a panel that included former Secretary of State Henry Kissinger, future National Security Advisor Brent Scowcroft, former Secretary of Defense Robert McNamara and others, hosted by Ted Koppel of ABC News. Shultz told Koppel that *The Day After* was "a vivid and

President Reagan and General Secretary Gorbachev signing the INF Treaty at the White House, December 8, 1987. *Courtesy of www.wikimedia.org.*

dramatic portrayal of the fact that nuclear war is simply not acceptable," and that the United States possessed its stockpile of nuclear weapons to deter war. Secretary Shultz also said that the United States intended to pursue a policy of not just reducing its nuclear arsenal but, hopefully, eliminating it.[208]

The INF Treaty eliminating intermediate range missiles was a move in that direction and a move toward ending decades-long conflict between the world's two superpowers. Gorbachev ultimately recognized the significance of the INF Treaty, its paving the way for peace between the two nations and an end to more than forty years of hostility that had endangered the world. He wrote in his memoir that the "INF Treaty represented the first well-prepared step on our way out of the Cold War."[209]

The movie's opening credits include these words: "We are grateful to the people of Lawrence, Kansas, for their participation and help in the making of this film."[210] By his own admission, this film encouraged President Ronald Reagan to sign the historic 1987 INF Treaty that, according to Soviet leader Mikhail Gorbachev, helped bring about the end of the Cold War. Kansas was central to a movie that played a very important role in moving the world away from nuclear annihilation and toward peace.

8

COLD WAR LEGACY

The Cold War ended when the Soviet Union dissolved in 1991. That conflict between the United States and the democratic West against the Soviet Union and its satellites behind the Iron Curtain lasted more than four decades and left its imprint on the entire nation, including Kansas. With the introduction of nuclear weapons, the Cold War became increasingly dangerous as the world's two superpowers sought to defend themselves and advance their interests. According to Scott D. Hughes in *Encyclopedia of the Great Plains*, "As the ideological battles played out, technological advances in weaponry increased the threat of thermonuclear holocaust."[211]

Just three years after World War II ended, the Strategic Air Command (SAC) made Offutt Air Force Base near Omaha, Nebraska, its headquarters. "SAC served as the air arm of the nation's offensive strategy for waging nuclear war," wrote Hughes, "and it existed as an icon of American military power for the duration" of the decades-long Cold War. SAC expanded its presence in the middle of the country with "long-range bombers, such [as] the B-36 and B-52, planes that were capable of deployment into Soviet airspace." These bombers were supplanted in importance by intercontinental ballistic missiles such as the Atlas, which was deployed near air force bases in states that included Oklahoma, Texas and Kansas. These military installations and the missile sites attached to them "served as economic engines, providing well-paid and secure civilian support employment to local inhabitants in host communities."[212]

As discussed in chapter 2, though economically advantageous for the states and localities that built ICBM sites and housed the missiles, and militarily advantageous for the nation in defending the nation and deterring possible attack, building those sites proved dangerous. More than fifty people died while building ICBM sites across several states, including eight who died building Kansas Atlas and Titan sites. Additionally, two air force personnel died at the Rock Titan II site in 1978. These were not the only American Cold War fatalities.

Americans also died as a result of fighting hot wars to stop Communist aggression in Korea and Vietnam. Of the more than 36,000 Americans who died fighting in Korea, 429 were from Kansas.[213] Of the more than 58,000 Americans who lost their lives serving the United States in the Vietnam War, 627 were from Kansas.[214] Though the United States was never officially at war with the Soviet Union during the Cold War, that conflict inspired American involvement in war abroad and defense at home that cost thousands of American lives. For the loved ones of those Americans—including Kansans—who, in the enduring words of General Douglas MacArthur, "gave all that mortality could give," the loss is part of the Cold War's legacy.[215]

The economic cost to the nation was also high. According to *Encyclopedia of the Great Plains*, "By 1995, the costs associated with the cold war had exceeded $5 trillion."[216]

Another aspect of Kansas's Cold War legacy includes the discarded Nike Hercules antiaircraft and Atlas E and F and Titan II intercontinental ballistic missile sites. All the Atlas sites were sold after those programs were phased out in 1965. Some are owned by private individuals, while others are owned by school districts. People even live in some of those ICBM sites. Useable equipment was removed from the Titan II sites after they were inactivated, and the empty silos were dynamited and filled.[217]

Anyone willing to pay the asking price would likely be able to buy an abandoned ICBM site. In 2017, an Atlas F site in New York was listed for sale. In 1997, it was purchased for $160,000, but in 2015 it was sold for $575,000. The 2017 asking price was $3 million. An Atlas site near Topeka was sold in the 1980s for $48,000, and the 2017 asking price was $3.2 million.[218]

As the nation implemented civil defense measures to survive a nuclear attack, Kansans sprang into action. Public fallout shelters were identified and stocked, home shelters were built and local civil defense units formed and planned for the unimaginable. College campuses prepared to survive nuclear attack, while at least one university hired a man to travel the state to educate Kansans in the science and art of nuclear survival. Even elementary-aged 4-H students were educated about civil defense. Another part of Kansas's Cold War legacy is buildings that once held fallout shelter signs and home shelters now used for storage and protection from severe weather. Civil defense preparedness, like nuclear deterrence, also cost. In the words of Hughes, states like Kansas "emerged from its cold war experience with deep ties to the federal defense budget, and with fallout shelters now used for storing canned goods and for refuge from tornadoes."[219]

The Cold War ended without a nuclear holocaust endangering civilization. As with any event that fades with the passing of time, the Cold War is a distant memory to some and nothing more than an era known only through history books by those too young to remember. It was, however, a dangerous time for Kansas, the nation and the world. Fortunately, through the leadership of Presidents Truman, Eisenhower, Kennedy and others, nuclear war was averted more than once, as rational men chose peace over war and life over national death in several crises. Our task is to remember the sacrifices, the stakes, the failures and the successes—to learn from the prologue that is our past as we chart our future

The Cold War began with uncertainty. Nobody knew how long it would last and if it would end peacefully or amid the ruins of a nuclear conflagration. The American foreign policy that guided the nation through the Cold War was begun under President Truman and, in large measure, continued by all future Cold War presidents, Democrat and Republican. Having lived through the entire Cold War, Clark Clifford, former counsel to President Truman, wrote these words about that policy in the early 1990s: "The policy that truly succeeded was born…when, in less than three years, President Truman unveiled the Truman Doctrine, the Marshall Plan, [and] NATO." Then, in the course of "the next forty years, the essential core of President Truman's policies survived…the four great challenges of…the Korean War, McCarthyism, Vietnam, and Watergate—and was accepted as the framework of our foreign policy by every President from Eisenhower to [George H.W.] Bush."[220]

Kansas's Cold War contributions were many. In fact, an argument can be made that Kansas's Cold War efforts were among the nation's most important. With three of the state's five military installations serving as hubs for intercontinental ballistic missiles, Kansas hosted more air force bases that operated ICBMs than any other state. The thirty-nine ICBMs deployed in Kansas during the 1960s were part of the nation's nuclear deterrent that moved Soviet leader Nikita Khrushchev to plead with

President Kennedy during the October 1962 Cuban Missile Crisis to pull back from the brink and avoid civilization-ending nuclear war. Among those thirty-nine ICBMs were eighteen Titan II missiles. The Titan II was the largest ICBM that the nation has ever utilized, and the nine-megaton warhead that each missile carried was the most powerful. Kansans were also featured in a movie filmed and set in Kansas that motivated President Reagan to sign the 1987 INF Treaty and move the world toward peace as the Cold War's end began. And in Dwight D. Eisenhower, Kansas provided one of only two Cold War U.S. presidents to serve two full terms. A soldier who succeeded like no other in waging war, Eisenhower was a president who succeeded equally well in waging peace.

Kansas and Kansans played key Cold War roles. As politicians, military personnel and civilians contributing to offensive preparedness, defensive preparedness and government domestic and foreign policy—and one important made-for-TV movie—Kansans are part of the nation's Cold War legacy. With three air force bases operating thirty-nine ICBMs, Kansans lived with the knowledge that the state was surely targeted by the Soviet Union and would be in the crosshairs of a nuclear attack. Kansans' efforts, the military installations that continue to operate in the state and those that do not, plus the former Nike sites and the abandoned Atlas and Titan missile silos and converted fallout shelters across the state, are all part of Kansas's Cold War legacy. This legacy is worth knowing. Kansas's Cold War role is worth remembering.

NOTES

Introduction

1. John F. Kennedy, "Address before the General Assembly of the United Nations, September 25, 1961," John F. Kennedy Presidential Library and Museum, www.jfklibrary.org.

Chapter 1

2. This chapter is reprinted from Landry Brewer's book *Cold War Oklahoma* (Charleston, SC: The History Press, 2019).
3. Stephen E. Ambrose and Douglas G. Brinkley, *Rise to Globalism: American Foreign Policy Since 1938* (London: Penguin Books, 2011), 53.
4. Ibid., 54–56.
5. "Churchill's Iron Curtain Speech," Westminster College, www. westminster-mo.edu.
6. Ambrose and Brinkley, *Rise to Globalism*, 76–82.
7. Ibid., 81, 83.
8. David McCullough, *Truman* (New York: Simon & Schuster, 1992), 582.
9. Ibid., 561–62.
10. Ibid., 562–63.

11. Ibid., 565, 583.
12. Ibid., 566.
13. Ambrose and Brinkley, *Rise to Globalism*, 98–99.
14. Richard Reeves, *Daring Young Men: The Heroism and Triumph of the Berlin Airlift, June 1948–May 1949* (New York: Simon & Schuster, 2010), 274.
15. Ambrose and Brinkley, *Rise to Globalism*, 101.
16. McCullough, *Truman*, 747–49.
17. Ibid., 742–44, 749.
18. Ibid., 749, 757, 761–63.
19. Ibid., 772; Ambrose and Brinkley, *Rise to Globalism*, 772.

Chapter 2

20. A portion of this chapter is reprinted from Landry Brewer's article "Kansas Missiles: Central Kansas and the Nation's Cold War Nuclear Arsenal, 1959–65," *Kansas History: A Journal of the Central Plains* 43, no. 1 (2020), with permission by the Kansas State Historical Society.
21. Evan Thomas, *Ike's Bluff: President Eisenhower's Secret Battle to Save the World* (New York: Little, Brown and Company, 2012), 15, 112–13; Stephen E. Ambrose, *Eisenhower: Soldier and President* (New York: Simon & Schuster, 1990), 356; John Lewis Gaddis, *The Cold War: A New History* (New York: Penguin Press, 2005), 66–67.
22. John C. Lonnquest and David F. Winkler, *To Defend and Deter: The Legacy of the United States Cold War Missile Program* (Washington, D.C.: U.S. Department of Defense, 1996), 65–66, www.atlasmissilesilo.com.
23. Ibid.
24. Ibid., 209–11.
25. Ibid., 77–78.
26. Ibid., 44, 79.
27. Ibid., 220, 341.
28. Ibid., 341.
29. Ibid., 220; U.S. Army Corps of Engineers [hereafter USACE], *History of Corps of Engineers Activities at Schilling Air Force Base, March 1960–December 1961* (Los Angeles: Corps of Engineers Ballistic Missile Construction Office, n.d.), 3-1, http://atlasmissilesilo.com.
30. Lonnquest and Winkler, *Defend and Deter*, 80–88; USACE, *History of Corps of Engineers*, 1-1, 2-1.
31. Lonnquest and Winkler, *Defend and Deter*, 68–69, 220.

32. "Sites Selected For Salina Area's Atlas Installations," *Salina (KS) Journal*, May 13, 1959.

33. Lonnquest and Winkler, *Defend and Deter*, 343–44.

34. Ibid., 83.

35. Ibid., 95–97.

36. "Students Protest Missile Base Near McPherson," *Salina (KS) Journal*, May 6, 1960.

37. Preston Grover, "Red Says Pilot Confessed, May Charge Him as a Spy," *Salina (KS) Journal*, May 8, 1960.

38. "Atlas Missile Sites Picked Near Three More Area Cities," *Salina (KS) Journal*, May 29, 1960.

39. Lonnquest and Winkler, *Defend and Deter*, 82.

40. USACE, *History of Corps of Engineers*, 24-1; "McPherson Missile Mishap Kills Missourian," *Salina (KS) Journal*, July 24, 1960.

41. "Will 600-Vote Dole Lead Stand?" *Salina (KS) Journal*, August 3, 1960.

42. "Crash Kills Hays Youth," *Salina (KS) Journal*, August 4, 1960; USACE, *History of Corps of Engineers*, 24-2–24-3.

43. "Missile Worker Killed in Fall," *Salina (KS) Journal*, October 10, 1960; USACE, *History of Corps of Engineers*, 24-3–24-4.

44. "Steel Worker Killed in Fall at Atlas Site," *Salina (KS) Journal*, November 20, 1960; USACE, *History of Corps of Engineers*, 24-4–24-5.

45. "Was Fatal Pipe Without Support?" *Salina (KS) Journal*, January 8, 1960; USACE, *History of Corps of Engineers*, 24-6.

46. USACE, *History of Corps of Engineers*, 24-7.

47. Thomas, *Ike's Bluff*, 407.

48. Ibid., 358.

49. Robert Dallek, *An Unfinished Life: John F. Kennedy, 1917–1963* (Boston: Little, Brown and Company, 2003), 347.

50. "Special Message to Congress on Urgent National Needs," quoted in B. Wayne Blanchard, *American Civil Defense 1945–1984: The Evolution of Programs and Policies*, Monograph Series 1985, vol. 2, no. 2 (Emmitsburg, MD: National Emergency Training Center, 1986), 7–8, www.civildefensemuseum.com.

51. "Cuba Invaded: Liberation Fight Opens," *Salina (KS) Journal*, April 17, 1961; "Russia Threatens to Give Military Help to Castro," *Salina (KS) Journal*, April 17, 1961.

52. "12 Area Missile Bases Presented to Air Force," *Salina (KS) Journal*, June 16, 1961.

53. "Atlas Missile Silos in Air Force Hands," *Salina (KS) Journal*, June 18, 1961.

54. Henry B. Jameson, "Atlas Missile Bases Turned Over to Military, Putting Abilene in the 'Target Area,'" *Abilene (KS) Daily Reflector-Chronicle*, June 17, 1961.

55. Ibid.

56. "West Will Bolster European Defenses in a Reply to Khrush's Threats," *Salina (KS) Journal*, June 23, 1961; "An Early Berlin Showdown Seen," *Salina (KS) Journal*, June 23, 1961; Gaddis, *Cold War*, 114–15.

57. Lewis Gulick, "U.S. Views Berlin Crisis with Alarm," *Salina (KS) Journal*, June 25, 1961.

58. "Missile Bases Prime Targets," *Salina (KS) Journal*, October 25, 1961.

59. "Atom Survival Briefing Open to Salinans," *Salina (KS) Journal*, October 18, 1961.

60. "Red Superbomb Maybe Even Bigger Than 50 Megatons," *Salina (KS) Journal*, October 30, 1961.

61. "Salina's Massive Missiles Ready," *Salina (KS) Journal*, September 13, 1962.

62. Strategic Air Command, *SAC Missile Chronology: 1939–1988* (Offutt AFB, NE: Office of the Historian, 1990), 37, www.siloworld.net.

63. "Shouting but No Shooting: Russia Rattles Rockets, However," *Salina (KS) Journal*, October 23, 1962.

64. "Schilling Mum on Alert Status," *Salina (KS) Journal*, October 23, 1962.

65. Strategic Air Command, *SAC Missile Chronology*, 40, 43–44.

66. Jacob Neufeld, *The Development of Ballistic Missiles in the United States Air Force 1945–1960* (U.S. Air Force, 1990), 233, 237, https://media.defense.gov; Lonnquest and Winkler, *Defend and Deter*, 342.

67. Lonnquest and Winkler, *Defend and Deter*, 92–94, 137; "First Schilling Missile Leaves for New Base," *Salina (KS) Journal*, January 5, 1965.

68. "Flood Extends Missile Crew's Duty Tour," *Salina (KS) Journal*, June 27, 1965.

69. "15 Bid on Atlas Silo Salvage Job," *Salina (KS) Journal*, December 1, 1965.

70. Lonnquest and Winkler, *Defend and Deter*, 4, 70–71.

71. Ibid., 70, 227–33; "The Titan Missile," U.S. National Park Service, www.nps.gov.

72. Lonnquest and Winkler, *Defend and Deter*, 342.

73. Ibid., 237–38.

74. Ibid., 342.

75. Ibid., 343; "Titan II Accident McConnell AFB, Kansas 1978," *Military Standard*, www.themilitarystandard.com.

76. Lonnquest and Winkler, *Defend and Deter*, 2–3, 29, 55, 57.

77. Ibid., 97, 99, 177, 181–82.

78. Ibid., 182, 344–45, 492.

79. "Nike Middle School Has Interesting History," *Gardner (KS) News*, August 30, 2015.
80. Quentin Schillare, "Post Once Home of Nike Missile Battery," *Fort Leavenworth Lamp*, December 15, 2016.
81. Neufeld, *Development of Ballistic Missiles*, 244.
82. Thomas, *Ike's Bluff*, 414.
83. "Department of State Telegram Transmitting Letter from Chairman Khrushchev to President Kennedy, October 26, 1962," John F. Kennedy Presidential Library and Museum, https://microsites.jfklibrary.org/cmc/oct26/doc4.html.
84. Michael Dobbs, *One Minute to Midnight: Kennedy, Khrushchev, and Castro on the Brink of Nuclear War* (New York: Vintage Books, 2008) 98–99, 189, 386.

Chapter 3

85. "Swords into Plowshares," *Impact: Kansas State Engineering Newsletter* 2, no. 1 (November 1966). https://engg.ksu.edu/docs/impact/archive/impact-fall-1966.pdf.
86. Ibid.
87. Byron W. Jones, interview by the author via email, October 8, 2019.
88. Ibid.
89. "Old Missile Sites Still Get Attention," *Wichita (KS) Eagle*, November 22, 2009; "Once a Missile Tunnel," *Grass & Grain*, December 9, 1969.
90. "Luxury Converted Kansas Nuclear Missile Silo Is Now Listed on Airbnb," Associated Press, November 27, 2017.
91. India Yarborough, "Kansas Couple Plans to Transform Atlas F Missile Silo," *U.S. News & World Report*, August 2, 2019.
92. Melia Robinson, "This 15-Story Underground Soomsday Shelter for the 1% Has Luxury Homes, Guns, and Armored trucks," *Business Insider*, August 24, 2018.
93. Ibid.
94. "Nike Middle School Has Interesting History," *Gardner (KS) News*, August 30, 2015.
95. Quentin Schillare, "Post Once Home of Nike Missile Bttery," *Fort Leavenworth Lamp*, December 15, 2016.

Chapter 4

96. Blanchard, *American Civil Defense*, 2–3; www.civildefensemuseum.com.

97. "Civil Defense Telephone," Kansapedia–Kansas Historical Society, www.kshs.org.

98. Ibid.

99. "Reasonably Safe—Kansas City's Civil Defense Drill," KC History, https://kchistory.org.

100. Ibid.

101. Ibid.

102. Ibid.

103. Scott D. Hughes, "Cold War," In *Encyclopedia of the Great Plains* (Lincoln: University of Nebraska, 2011), http://plainshumanities.unl.edu.

104. Ibid., 4–6; U.S. Department of Homeland Security [hereafter USDHS], *Civil Defense and Homeland Security: A Short History of National Preparedness Efforts* (Homeland Security National Preparedness Task Force, 2006), 9–10, https://raining.fema.gov.

105. Blanchard, *American Civil Defense*, 6–7.

106. Thomas, *Ike's Bluff*, 270, 272–74.

107. Ibid., 274.

108. "'Black Cloud' Starts CD Operation Alert," *Salina (KS) Journal*, May 3, 1960.

109. "Civil Defense Food Kit," Kansapedia–Kansas Historical Society, www.kshs.org.

110. "Special Message to Congress on Urgent National Needs," quoted in Blanchard, *American Civil Defense*, 7–8.

111. Blanchard, *American Civil Defense*, 8.

112. "Reno County Civil Defense Shelter," Kansapedia–Kansas Historical Society, www.kshs.org.

113. James Gregory, "In the Fallout Shelter: Civil Defense in Stillwater," *Stillwater Living Magazine*, October 11, 2017, 3–4, http://stillwaterliving.com.

114. USDHS, *Civil Defense and Homeland Security*, 12.

115. "Atom Survival Briefing Open to Salinans," *Salina (KS) Journal*, October 18, 1961.

116. "Ike Would Walk Out of Fallout Shelter If Family Not with Him," *Salina (KS) Journal*, October 18, 1961.

117. "To Escape the Fallout Go Live in the Desert," *Salina (KS) Journal*, October 18, 1961.

118. "Missile Bases Prime Targets," *Salina (KS) Journal*, October 25, 1961.

119. Elton Fay, "The Military Being Urged to Build Fallout Shelters," *Salina (KS) Journal*, October 30, 1961.

120. "No New Shelter Program Started at Schilling," *Salina (KS) Journal*, October 30, 1961.

121. "But Salina's Evacuation Route Signs Will Remain," *Salina (KS) Journal*, November 1, 1961.

122. "This Advice May Save Your Life," *Salina (KS) Journal*, November 3, 1961.

123. Willard F. Libby, "You Can Survive Atomic Attack—2: 95 Percent Can Survive," *Salina (KS) Journal*, November 7, 1961.

124. Willard F. Libby, "You Can Survive Atomic Attack—No. 4: Here Are Tips on Building Cheap Shelter," *Salina (KS) Journal*, November 8, 1961.

125. "Topeka Man to Rent Space in Fallout Shelter," *Salina (KS) Journal*, November 8, 1961.

126. Willard F. Libby, "You Can Survive Atomic Attack—No. 5: The Better The Shelter The Better Your Chances," *Salina (KS) Journal*, November 9, 1961.

127. Willard F. Libby, "You Can Survive Atomic Attack—No. 7: Yes, You Might Have Time to Get Home to Shelter," *Salina (KS) Journal*, November 14, 1961.

128. Willard F. Libby, "You Can Survive Nuclear Attack—No. 12: Tell Children Simple Facts About Nuclear Attack," *Salina (KS) Journal*, November 21, 1961.

129. "Assistant Professor Converts RR Water Tank into Shelter," *Kansas State Collegian*, December 6, 1961.

130. Elton Fay, "Fallout Survival Booklet to Be Distributed," *Salina (KS) Journal*, December 31, 1961.

131. Office of Civil Defense, *Family Shelter Designs*, (Washington, D.C.: U.S. Department of Defense, 1962), 2–29.

132. "Community Fallout Shelter Supplies—Water Storage Drums," Civil Defense Museum, www.civildefensemuseum.com.

133. Office of Civil Defense, *Federal Civil Defense Guide* (Washington, D.C.: U.S. Department of Defense, 1964) part D, chapter 2, appendix 6, "Fallout Shelter Food Requirements," 1–2. www.civildefensemuseum.com.

134. Ibid., part D, chapter 2, appendix 8, "Fallout Shelter Medical Kit," 1–2.

135. "Variety Show Raises $600 for CD Fund," *Salina (KS) Journal*, April 2, 1962.

136. "CD Activity Is Stepped Up," *Salina (KS) Journal*, October 28, 1962.

137. "Fallout Shelter Plan Urged by CD Officials," *Salina (KS) Journal*, February 1, 1966.

138. "CD Activity Is Stepped Up," *Salina (KS) Journal*, October 28, 1962.

139. "Scottsville Farmer Leaves Little to Fate or Chance," *Salina (KS) Journal*, November 25, 1962.

140. "Stress Local Responsibility at CD Seminar," *Salina (KS) Journal*, December 16, 1963.

141. "CD Speaker Test July 9," *Salina (KS) Journal*, June 28, 1964.

142. "CD Okays 20 Shelters," *Kansas State Collegian*, March 30, 1965.

143. "Campus Whistle—Civil Defense Warning," *Kansas State Collegian*, April 30, 1965.

144. "4-H'ERS LEARN OF CIVIL DEFENSE," *Kansas 4-H Journal*, July 1966, https://krex.k-state.edu.

145. Rosanna Vail, "PROTECTING THE PEOPLE: Education That Kept Kansans Safe in Turbulent Times," *Kansas State University Global Campus–LINK*, Fall/Winter 2016, 4–5, https://global.k-state.edu.

146. Blanchard, *American Civil Defense*, 11–12, 14–15; USDHS, *Civil Defense and Homeland Security*, 13–14.

147. Mike Matson, "Growing up in Kansas, I'm Finely Attuned to the Postapocalypse," *The Mercury*, June 30, 2019.

Chapter 5

148. Ambrose, *Eisenhower*, 15, 22, 28–35; "The Eisenhowers: Dwight David Eisenhower Chronology," Dwight D. Eisenhower Presidential Library, www.eisenhowerlibrary.gov/eisenhowers.

149. Ambrose, *Eisenhower*, 41–44, 51, 56–58, 60–61, 65.

150. Ibid., 70–71, 74–78, 80–82, 91, 113–16, 127, 139–41, 192, 199–203; "Eisenhowers."

151. Ambrose, *Eisenhower*, 204–5, 228–29, 232–33, 264–65, 272–73, 285–87.

152. Ibid., 296–97.

153. Ibid., 311, 323–26.

154. Ibid., 328–31.

155. Ibid., 338.

156. Ibid., 342–43.

157. Ibid., 321, 356–57.

158. Ibid., 357–63, 368–71; Thomas, *Ike's Bluff*, 127.

159. Ambrose, *Eisenhower*, 377–78; Thomas, *Ike's Bluff*, 147–51.

160. Ambrose, *Eisenhower*, 369–70, 379, 383; Thomas, *Ike's Bluff*, 135.

161. Ambrose, *Eisenhower*, 389–93; Thomas, *Ike's Bluff*, 172–79.

162. Thomas, *Ike's Bluff*, 167.

163. Ambrose, *Eisenhower*, 410–11.
164. David A. Nichols, *Eisenhower 1956: The President's Year of Crisis—Suez and the Brink of War* (New York: Simon & Schuster, 2011), 56, 64–65, 157; Thomas, *Ike's Bluff*, 198.
165. Ambrose, *Eisenhower*, 415–33; Thomas, *Ike's Bluff*, 216–24, 228–34.
166. Ambrose, *Eisenhower*, 448–54, 461; Thomas, *Ike's Bluff*, 252–56.
167. Ambrose, *Eisenhower*, 478; Thomas, *Ike's Bluff*, 314–15.
168. Ambrose, *Eisenhower*, 481–84, 487; Thomas, *Ike's Bluff*, 318–31.
169. Ambrose, *Eisenhower*, 475, 500, 517, 538.
170. Ibid., 502–4; Thomas, *Ike's Bluff*, 358, 360.
171. Ambrose, *Eisenhower*, 504–14; Thomas, *Ike's Bluff*, 369–79, 381–83.
172. Ambrose, *Eisenhower*, 536–37.
173. Thomas, *Ike's Bluff*, 16, 416.
174. Ambrose, *Eisenhower*, 566, 571, 574.

Chapter 6

175. "The History of Forbes Field," 190th Air Refueling Wing, www.190arw. ang.af.mil.
176. Ibid.
177. Ibid.
178. Ibid.; Tim Hrenchir, "Economically, Air Base Had Topeka Flying High," *Topeka Capital-Journal*, April 20, 2013.
179. Hrenchir, "Economically, Air Base Had Topeka Flying High."
180. "History and Missions of Fort Leavenworth," U.S. Army Bases, http:// armybases.org.
181. "Fort Riley, KS History," www.ftrileyhousing.com/history
182. "History of Fort Riley," U.S. Army Bases, http://armybases.org.
183. "Fort Riley, KS History."
184. Ibid.; "History of Fort Riley."
185. *Heritage and Legacy: A Brief History of the 22nd Air Refueling Wing and McConnell Air Force Base* (McConnell AFB, KS: Office of History 2017), 38–39, www.mcconnell.af.mil; "McConnell Air Force Base: McConnell's History," United States Air Force, www.mcconnell.af.mil.
186. *Heritage and Legacy*, 28–31.
187. "Welcome to Schilling Air Force Base," United States Air Force, www. siloworld.net.
188. Ibid., 3, 8–9.

189. Gordon D. Fielder Jr., "The Closing of Schilling Air Force Base," *Salina (KS) Journal*, November 16, 2014, www.salina.com.

190. Donald W. Lorenzo, "Some Aspects of the Economic Impact of Closing Schilling Air Force Base, Salina, Kansas" (Master's report, Kansas State University, 1966), 5, 12–13, 16–17, 20, 22, https://krex.k-state.edu.

191. Ibid., 25–26.

192. Ibid., 28, 30, 33–34.

193. Ibid., 38, 41, 44.

194. Fielder, "Closing of Schilling Air Force Base."

Chapter 7

195. Sean O'Neal, "*The Day After* Traumatized a Generation with the Horrors of Nuclear War," *AV Club*, August 28, 2017, www.avclub.com; Jason Roe, "KC History: Going Nuclear," Kansas City Public Library, https://kchistory.org.

196. O'Neal, "*The Day After*."

197. Roe, "KC History."

198. Ibid.

199. Dawn Stover, "Facing Nuclear Reality 35 Years after *The Day After*," *Bulletin of the Atomic Scientists*, https://thebulletin.org.

200. Ibid.

201. O'Neal, "*The Day After*."

202. Stover, "Facing Nuclear Reality."

203. O'Neal, "*The Day After*."

204. Ibid.; Stover, "Facing Nuclear Reality."

205. Stover, "Facing Nuclear Reality."

206. Ibid.

207. Quoted in Stover, "Facing Nuclear Reality."

208. Ibid.

209. Quoted in James Mann, *The Rebellion of Ronald Reagan: A History of the End of the Cold War* (New York: Viking, 2009), 277.

210. Stover, "Facing Nuclear Reality."

Chapter 8

211. Scott D. Hughes, "Cold War," *Encyclopedia of the Great Plains*, University of Nebraska Lincoln http://plainshumanities.unl.edu.
212. Ibid.
213. "U.S. Military Fatal Casualties of the Korean War for Home-State-of-Record: Kansas," National Archives Web Site, www.archives.gov.
214. "U.S. Military Fatal Casualties of the Vietnam War for Home-State-of-Record: Kansas," National Archives Web Site, https://www.archives.gov.
215. Douglas MacArthur, "Duty, Honor, Country," Jackson State University, May 12, 1962, www.jsums.edu.
216. Hughes, "Cold War."
217. Lonnquest and Winkler, *Defend and Deter*, 306.
218. Colleen Kane, "7 Doomsday Bunkers for Surviving the Apocalypse, No Matter Your Budget," *Time*, http://time.com.
219. Hughes, "Cold War."
220. Clark Clifford and Richard Holbrooke, *Counsel to the President: A Memoir* (New York: Random House, 1991), 660.

ABOUT THE AUTHOR

Landry Brewer is Bernhardt Assistant Professor of History for Southwestern Oklahoma State University and teaches at the Sayre campus. Brewer is also the author of *Cold War Oklahoma*.

He and his wife, Erin, have five children and live in Elk City.

Visit us at
www.historypress.com
···